Editor
Mary S. Jones, M.A.

Illustrator
Kevin McCarthy

Cover Artist
Brenda DiAntonis

Managing Editor
Ina Massler Levin, M.A.

Creative Director
Karen J. Goldfluss, M.S. Ed.

Art Production Manager
Kevin Barnes

Art Coordinator
Renée Christine Yates

Imaging
Rosa C. See

Publisher

Mary D. Smith, M.S. Ed.

W9-AMP-425

Document-Based Questions

for Reading Comprehension and Critical Thinking

Grade 3

Author

Debra J. Housel, M.S. Ed.

Correlations to the Common Core
State Standards can be found at
http://www.teachercreated.com/standards/.

Teacher Created Resources, Inc.
12621 Western Avenue
Garden Grove, CA 92841
www.teachercreated.com
ISBN: 978-1-4206-8373-8
©2007 Teacher Created Resources, Inc.
Reprinted, 2016
Made in U.S.A.

Teacher Created Resources

Table of Contents

Introduction

About This Book. 3

Applying Bloom's Taxonomy. 4

Practice Suggestions. 7

Standardized Test Success 8

Standards and Benchmarks. 9

Interesting Plants and Animals

Birds that Swim Instead of Fly. 10

The Venus Flytrap. 13

The Peculiar Platypus 16

Kelp: The Underwater Forest 19

Cheetahs Are Fast Cats. 22

Poisonous Plants: Good or Bad? 25

Great Adventures and Rescues

Around the World in 72 Days. 28

The Search for the Northwest Passage. 31

The Great Race of Mercy 34

Daring Rescue During the Buffalo Blizzard
  of 1977 37

Stranded Near a Mountaintop. 40

A Monster Wave Flips Two Boats 43

Trapped Underground! 46

Incredible Disasters

Krakatau, a Deadly Volcano 49

Destructive Wind and Water: The Galveston
  Hurricane 52

The Dust Bowl 55

Avalanche! 58

Flash Flood in Big Thompson Canyon. 61

Deadly Cloud from Lake Nyos. 64

Amazing Discoveries and Inventions

Gunpowder Inventions 67

The Miracle of Movable Type 70

Galileo's Discoveries About the Universe 73

Dinosaurs 76

Joseph Lister's Fight Against Germs 79

The Janitor's Invention. 82

Did You Know?

Recycling 85

Earth's Hot Spots .88

Big Blast in Siberia. 91

The Story of the Brooklyn Bridge 94

Libraries Make the World a Smarter Place. 97

Lightships 100

Mount Rushmore .103

Answer Key 106

About This Book

The primary goal of any reading task is comprehension. *Document-Based Questions for Reading Comprehension and Critical Thinking* uses high-interest grade-level nonfiction passages, related documents, and critical thinking assessment practice to help you develop confident readers who can demonstrate their skills on standardized tests. In addition, you will build the comprehension skills necessary for a lifetime of learning.

There are five topic areas with six or seven lessons in each. Each lesson consists of three pages: a reading passage, a related document, and an assessment practice page containing multiple choice, true-false-explain, and short-answer document-based questions. This gives your students practice in all of the question types used in standardized testing. The students respond to the document-based questions based on the information gleaned from the passage plus its related document. Such questions improve a student's ability to apply prior knowledge, integrate information, and transfer knowledge to a new situation.

Readability

These passages have a 3.0–3.9 reading level based on the Flesch Kincaid Readability Formula. This formula, built into *Microsoft® Word™*, determines readability by calculating the number of words, syllables, and sentences. Average readability was determined for each of the five topic areas. The topics are presented in order of increasing difficulty.

The documents are not leveled. Many of them are historical pieces and therefore replicated with the exact wording. Some terminology may be challenging, but most students can handle difficult words within the context given.

Preparing Students to Read Nonfiction Text

One of the best ways to prepare students to read expository text is to read a short selection aloud to them daily. Reading expository text aloud is critical to developing your students' ability to read it themselves. Since making predictions is another way to make students tap into their prior knowledge, read the beginning of a passage, then stop, and ask them to predict what might occur next. Do this at several points throughout your reading of the text. By doing this, over time you will find that your students' ability to make accurate predictions increases.

Your questions will help students, especially struggling readers, focus on what's important in a text. Also, remember the significance of wait time. Research has shown that the amount of time an educator waits for a student to answer after posing a question has a critical effect on learning. So after you ask a student a question, silently count to five (ten if you have a student who really struggles to put his or her thoughts into words) before giving any additional prompts or redirecting the question to another student.

Talking about nonfiction concepts is also important. Remember, however, that discussion can never replace reading aloud because people rarely speak using the vocabulary and complex sentence structures of written language.

Applying Bloom's Taxonomy

The questions on the assessment practice pages in *Document-Based Questions for Reading Comprehension and Critical Thinking* assess all levels of learning in Bloom's Taxonomy. Benjamin Bloom devised this six-level classification system for comprehension questions. The questions on each assessment practice passage are always presented in this order. They progress from easiest to most challenging.

- **Level 1: Knowledge**—Students recall information or can find requested information in an article. They recognize dates, events, places, people, and main ideas.
- **Level 2: Comprehension**—Students understand information. This means that they can find information that is stated in a different way than the question. It also means students can rephrase or restate information in their own words.
- **Level 3: Application**—Students apply their knowledge to a specific situation. They may be asked to do something new with the knowledge.
- **Level 4: Analysis**—Students break things into their component parts and examine those parts. They notice patterns in information.
- **Level 5: Synthesis**—Students do something new with the information. They integrate knowledge and create new ideas. They generalize, predict, plan, and draw conclusions.
- **Level 6: Evaluation**—Students make judgments and assess value. They form an opinion and defend it. They can also understand another person's viewpoint.

These skills are essential to keep in mind when teaching comprehension to assure that your students practice the higher levels of thinking. Use this classification to form your own questions whenever your students read or listen to material.

Assessment Practice Pages

Teach your students to read the passage and its related document before answering any of the questions on the assessment practice page. Armed with this information, your students can more rapidly and accurately answer each question.

Multiple Choice Questions

The first three questions are multiple choice. Based solely on the information given in the passage, they cover the knowledge, comprehension, and application levels of Bloom's taxonomy.

For these questions, demonstrate your own thought process by doing a "think aloud" to figure out an answer. Tell your students your thoughts as they come to you. For example, suppose the question was: "In Yellowstone National Park, grizzly bears (a) do tricks, (b) roam free, or (c) get caught in traps."

Tell the students all your thoughts as they occur to you:

"Well, the grizzly bears living in Yellowstone National Park are wild bears. So of course they don't do tricks. So I'll get rid of choice A. That leaves me with 'roam free' or 'get caught in traps.' Let me look back at the passage and see what it says about traps." (Refer back to article.)

Applying Bloom's Taxonomy *(cont.)*

Multiple Choice Questions *(cont.)*

"I don't see anything about traps in the passage. And I did see that it says that in Yellowstone National Park the bears are protected and their population is increasing. That means they're safe from traps, which are dangerous. So I'm going to select (b) roam free."

True-False-Explain Questions

The fourth question is true-false-explain. It tests the analysis level of Bloom's taxonomy. This question may require students to use information from both the passage and the document to generate an answer. Just a one- or two-sentence response is required. To respond correctly, the student must not only distinguish facts from falsehoods but also explain them. This requires logical reasoning and analytical thinking. They cannot receive full credit without an adequate explanation. You must demonstrate how to write a good explanation. For example, in response to the statement, "Thomas Jefferson wrote the Gettysburg Address," the students could write, "False. Abraham Lincoln wrote the Gettysburg Address" OR "False. Thomas Jefferson wrote the Declaration of Independence." Either answer is acceptable and worth full credit.

When the statement is clearly true, the student must state that and add information. For example, in response to the statement, "Early pioneers in the Midwest had to cope with grasshopper plagues," the students should write, "True. The grasshoppers destroyed crops and even damaged buildings."

Make sure that your students know that sometimes both true and false responses can be correct. For example, in an article about rescuing Jewish children from the Warsaw Ghetto, it states how hard it was to convince the parents to let the rescue organization take away their children. It also details the methods used to get the kids past the guards (crawling through sewers, sedated babies in toolboxes). In response to the question, "During the rescue operation, the most difficult part was getting the parents to release their kids to the rescuers," some students may respond "True. Many parents did not want to let their children go. They were not sure that the children were in danger and thought that they could protect them." But others may say, "False. The hardest part was getting the kids out of the Ghetto without the Gestapo discovering what was going on."

Either response is worth full credit because it is adequately defended. This promotes critical thinking since the students must digest the information in order to take a stance.

Document-Based Questions

The remaining questions require the students to integrate the information provided in the passage with the information shown in the document. You must guide your students in understanding and responding to the document-based questions. Again, the best way to teach such skills is to demonstrate the formulation of an answer through a think aloud.

Applying Bloom's Taxonomy (cont.)

Short-Answer Questions

The fifth and sixth questions test the synthesis and evaluative levels of Bloom's taxonomy. Synthesis questions make your students draw conclusions based on information gleaned from both the passage and its document. Their response requires only a few sentences. Show your students how to restate the words from the question to formulate a cogent response. For example, in response to "Why were some people against the building of the Hoover Dam?" the students could write, "Some people were against the building of the Hoover Dam because it backed up a river, forming a huge lake. Historical Native American sites were flooded and animals' homes destroyed."

The final short answer question will be evaluative—the highest level of Bloom's taxonomy. This means that it is an opinion statement with no right answer. Evaluative questions demand the highest thinking and logical reasoning skills. The child must take a stance and defend it. Although there is no correct response, it is critical that the students support their opinions using facts and logic. Show them a format for the defense—by stating their opinion followed by the word "because" and a reason. For example, have a student respond to this question, "Do you think that whales should be kept in aquariums and sea parks for people to enjoy?" The student may respond, "I do not think that whales should be kept at sea parks because they are wild animals and don't want to be there. They want to be free in the ocean." Do not award full credit unless the student adequately supports his or her opinion.

Sample defenses are given for the evaluative questions, but students may present other valid opinions as well. Also, it would be most effective if you used the defenses written by the students themselves. Thus, before passing back the practice papers, make note of two children who had opposing opinions. Then, during the wrap-up discussion, call on each of these students to read his or her defense to the class. If all the children had the same conclusion, give the opposing opinion from the answer key to show them both sides of the issue. When it's obvious that a topic has generated strong opinions in your students, you can encourage your class to debate.

Practice Suggestions

Read aloud the first passage in each of the five topic areas and answer its related questions with the whole class. Such group practice is essential. The more your students practice, the more competent and confident they will become. Plan to have your class do every exercise in the *Document-Based Questions for Reading Comprehension and Critical Thinking*. The activities are time-efficient so that your students can practice each week. To yield the best results, practice must begin at the start of the school year.

If you have some students who cannot read the articles independently, allow them to read with a partner, then work through the comprehension questions alone. Eventually all students must practice reading and answering the questions independently. Move to this stage as soon as possible. For the most effective practice sessions, follow these steps:

1. Have students read the text silently and answer the questions.

2. Have students exchange papers to correct each other's multiple choice section.

3. Collect all the papers to score the short answer questions.

4. Return the papers to their owners and discuss how the students determined their answers.

5. Refer to the exact wording in the passage.

6. Point out how students had to use their background knowledge to answer certain questions.

7. Discuss the document-based questions thoroughly. Do think-alouds to show how you integrated information from the passage and the document to formulate your response.

8. Discuss how a child should defend his or her stance in an evaluative short-answer question.

Scoring the Assessment Practice Pages

Multiple Choice Questions (3)	12 points each	36 points
True-False-Explain Question (1)	16 points	16 points
Short-Answer Questions (2)	24 points each	48 points
	Total	100 points

Standardized Test Success

A key objective of *Document-Based Questions for Reading Comprehension and Critical Thinking* is to prepare your students to get the best possible scores on standardized tests. You may want to practice environmental conditions throughout the year in order to get your students used to the testing environment. For example, if your students' desks are usually together, have students move them apart whenever you practice so it won't feel strange on the test day.

A student's ability to do well on traditional standardized tests on comprehension requires these good test-taking skills. Thus, every student in your class needs instruction in test-taking skills. Even fluent readers and logical thinkers will perform better on standardized tests if you provide instruction in these areas:

- **Understanding the question:** Teach students to break down the question to figure out what is really being asked of them. This book will prepare them for the kinds of questions they will encounter on standardized tests.

- **Concentrating on what the text says:** Show students how to restrict their response to just what is asked. When you go over the practice pages, ask your students to show where they found the correct response or inference in the text.

- **Ruling out distracters in multiple choice answers:** Teach students to look for the key words in a question and look for those specific words to find the information in the text. They also need to know that they may have to look for synonyms for the key words.

- **Maintaining concentration:** Use classroom time to practice this in advance. Reward students for maintaining concentration. Explain to them the purpose of this practice and the reason why concentration is so essential.

Students will need to use test-taking skills and strategies throughout their lives. The exercises in *Document-Based Questions for Reading Comprehension and Critical Thinking* will guide your students to become better readers and test-takers. After practicing the exercises in this book, you will be pleased with your students' comprehension performance, not only on standardized tests, but with any expository text they encounter—within the classroom and beyond its walls.

Standards and Benchmarks

Each passage and comprehension question in *Document-Based Questions* meets at least one of the following standards and benchmarks, which are used with permission from McREL. (Copyright 2010 McREL, Mid-continent Research for Education and Learning. Telephone: 303-337-0990. Website: *www.mcrel.org*). Visit *http://www.teachercreated.com/standards/* for correlations to the Common Core State Standards.

McREL Standards are in bold. Benchmarks are in regular print. All lessons meet the following standards and benchmarks.

STANDARD 5 **Uses the general skills and strategies of the reading process.**

Level II

Benchmark 3 Makes, confirms, and revises simple predictions about what will be found in a text (e.g., uses prior knowledge and ideas presented in text, illustrations, titles, topic sentences, key words, and foreshadowing clues)

Benchmark 7 Understands level-appropriate reading vocabulary (e.g., synonyms, antonyms, homophones, multi-meaning words)

Benchmark 10 Understands the author's purpose (e.g., to persuade, to inform) or point of view

STANDARD 7 **Uses reading skills and strategies to understand and interpret a variety of informational texts.**

Level II

Benchmark 1 Uses reading skills and strategies to understand a variety of informational texts (e.g., textbooks, biographical sketches, letters, diaries, directions, procedures, magazines)

Benchmark 5 Summarizes and paraphrases information in texts (e.g., includes the main idea and significant supporting details of a reading selection)

Benchmark 6 Uses prior knowledge and experience to understand and respond to new information

STANDARD 1 **Uses the general skills and strategies of the writing process.**
Level II

Benchmark 6 Uses strategies (e.g., adapts focus, point of view, organization, form) to write for a variety of purposes (e.g., to inform, entertain, explain, describe, record ideas)

Benchmark 7 Writes expository compositions (e.g., identifies and stays on the topic; develops the topic with simple facts, details, examples, and explanations; excludes extraneous and inappropriate information; uses structures such as cause-and-effect, chronology, similarities and differences; uses several sources of information; provides a concluding statement)

Birds that Swim Instead of Fly

Emperor penguins are birds. But they cannot fly. Instead they swim. They use their "wings" as flippers to move through the water. They swim in the icy seas around Antarctica. When they are in the water, they stay in big groups. They call to each other. Being in a group keeps them safer from the leopard seals that want to eat them, too.

Adult emperor penguins are about the same size as you. They are about four feet tall and weigh about 70 pounds. When penguins are on shore, they gather in big groups called rookeries. Rookeries may have thousands of penguins. There the penguins pick their mates.

In the winter, when it is dark and very, very cold, each mother penguin lays one egg on the ice. The father quickly pulls the egg into an opening near his feet called a broodpouch. Then the mothers leave to find fish, krill*, and squid to eat. They stay out at sea for two months. During that time all of the fathers stay close together to keep from getting too cold. They also have a layer of fat to keep them warm. They must stand over their eggs for two months without ever leaving them. During that time they eat no food. They must live off their body fat.

After the egg hatches, the chick stays in the father's broodpouch. This keeps it warm. At last the mothers return with food for the chicks. They spit up food they have eaten. They spit the food into the baby penguins' hungry mouths. Then their mothers tuck them into their own broodpouches. After four months the chicks can swim and get their own food.

*A krill is a tiny, shrimp-like crustacean.

10   ©*Teacher Created Resources, Inc.*

Birds that Swim Instead of Fly

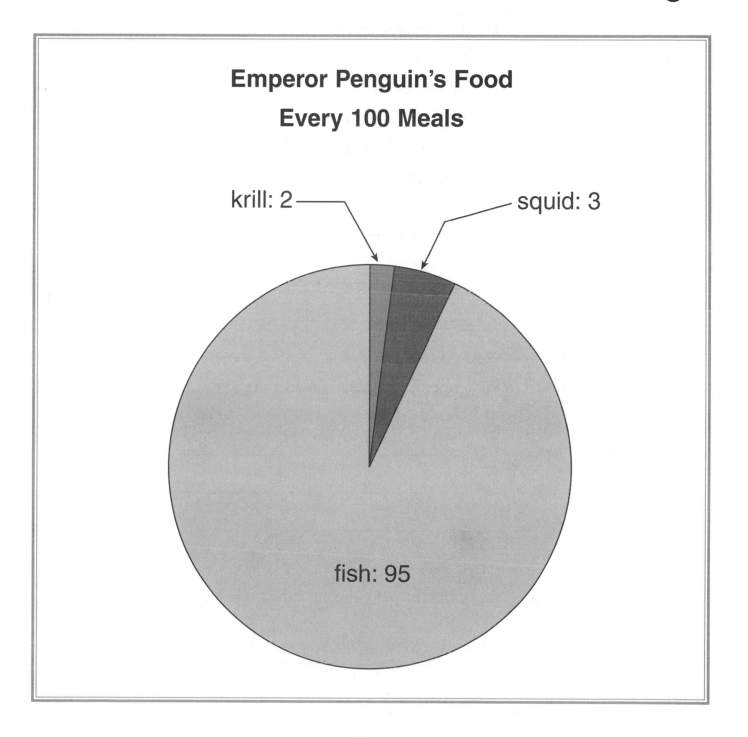

Emperor Penguin's Food
Every 100 Meals

krill: 2

squid: 3

fish: 95

Birds that Swim Instead of Fly

1. Which animal wants to eat the emperor penguin?

   a. leopard seal   b. krill   c. squid

2. How are emperor penguins like other birds?

   a. They fly.   b. They build nests.   c. They lay eggs.

3. What would the male penguin most likely do when his mate brings food for the baby?

   a. keeps the baby in his broodpouch   c. goes to sea to get his own food

   b. steals the baby's food

4. Emperor penguins eat more krill than any other food. True or False? Explain.

   _____

   _____

   _____

5. What would happen to the emperor penguins if something caused all of the squid in their area to die?

   _____

   _____

   _____

   _____

6. Do you think it's good that emperor penguins have just one baby each year? Why or why not?

   _____

   _____

   _____

The Venus Flytrap

Venus flytraps are plants that eat bugs! When people first discovered these plants, they took them home. Soon everyone wanted one. Many were taken from the wild for people to buy as houseplants. This made the plants endangered. Too few were left in the wild. Now it is against the law to take one from nature.

Like other plants, Venus flytraps take in nutrients from the soil. But they live in poor soil that lacks nitrogen. So they get the nitrogen from bugs and spiders. Venus flytraps live only in bogs in North and South Carolina. They also thrive in greenhouses.

The two halves of the trap of the Venus flytrap open wide. Each half has some short, stiff hairs. If something touches these hairs, the two sides of the trap slam shut in less than one second! At first the trap doesn't close tightly. This lets tiny bugs escape. Little bugs take more energy to digest than they would give to the plant.

The trap hairs must be touched two times fast. This is to keep it from being triggered by raindrops. Yet sometimes the trap closes on a stone or twig. When that happens, it reopens after 12 hours. Over time the thing gets washed away by rainfall or blown away by the wind.

When the trap does close on a bug, its cilia keep the animal inside. Cilia look like teeth lining the top edges of the trap. The cilia work like lacing your fingers together. Once the trap shuts, it forms a seal. This keeps digestive fluids in and germs out.

It takes the plant about 10 days to digest the bug. Then the trap reopens. Some parts of a bug cannot be digested. They remain when the trap reopens. Other times a bug is too big. It sticks out. This lets any germs or mold on the bug invade the trap. When this happens, the trap turns black. It falls off the stem. This protects the rest of the Venus flytrap from the disease.

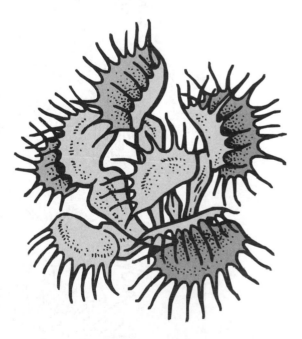

A Venus flytrap has many traps.

The Venus Flytrap

This diagram shows how a Venus flytrap traps and eats an insect.

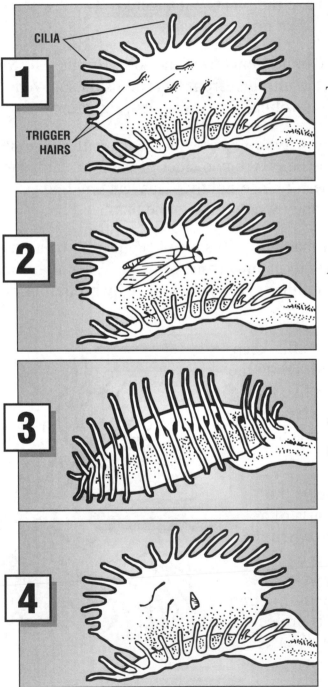

1. The trap is open.

2. An insect lands on the trap.

3. The trap closes on the insect and digests it.

4. The trap reopens. Some insect remains may be seen.

The Venus Flytrap

1. Where <u>won't</u> you find a Venus flytrap plant living in nature?

   a. Georgia   b. North Carolina   c. South Carolina

2. How long does it take the Venus flytrap to digest a bug?

   a. 12 hours   b. 1 week   c. 10 days

3. Which animal would the trap let escape instead of digest?

   a. an ant   b. a fly   c. a spider

4. The Venus flytrap has a way to keep from becoming diseased. True or False? Explain.

_____

_____

_____

5. Since both traps are open, how does step 1 differ from step 4?

_____

_____

_____

6. Would you like to have a Venus flytrap as a house plant? Why or why not?

_____

_____

_____

The Peculiar Platypus

A platypus is an odd mammal. It lives only in Australia. Its wide, flat tail and webbed feet make it a good swimmer. It scoops up worms and shellfish from stream bottoms with its wide, flat bill. It uses the claws on its feet to walk and to dig dirt. It digs long burrows along streams. Some are as long as 50 feet! Each one lives alone in its burrow.

Whenever it is underwater, the platypus closes its eyes and ears. So how does it find its food? It feels things with its bill. It is made of cartilage, just like our noses. Males have spurs on their hind feet. If a predator is kicked with the spur, it gets poisoned! The toxin is so strong that it can kill a dog and make people quite ill. Only four other mammals make poison. (They are all shrews, which look like moles.)

Adult platypuses are less than two feet long and weigh just five pounds. Their thick brown fur makes them look bigger. Hunters used to kill them for their fur. Their numbers dropped. People feared that they would die out. So since the 1920s, it has been against the law to kill one.

Unlike most mammals, the platypus lays eggs. The female uses grass and leaves to make a nest at the end of her burrow. Next she blocks the burrow's opening with dirt. Then she lays two or three eggs. Soon the babies hatch. They drink her milk for four months. Then they go out on their own.

Why is the platypus so different from other mammals? It developed away from other mammals. Long ago the land of Australia broke free from a bigger continent. It slowly drifted to its current spot. The platypuses on Australia slowly changed over time. But they developed differently from other mammals because they were in a unique environment.

The Peculiar Platypus

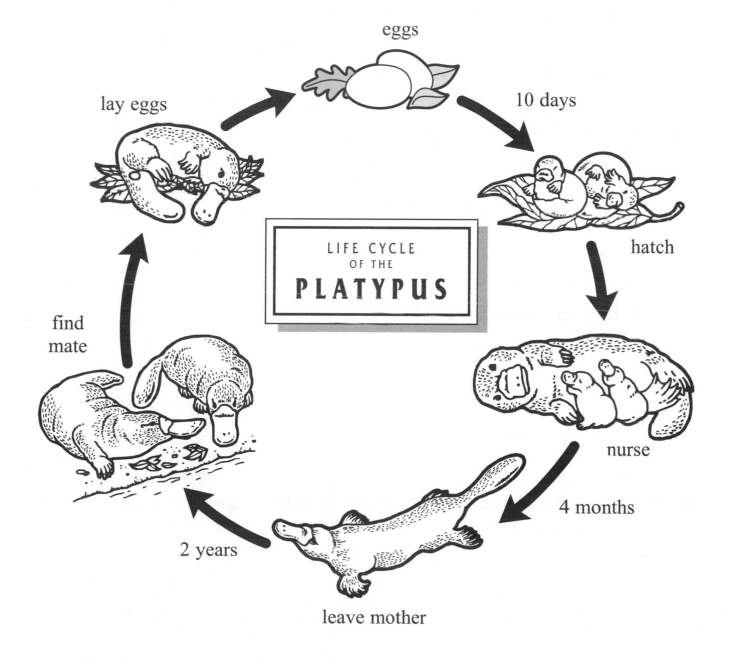

eggs

lay eggs

10 days

hatch

LIFE CYCLE
OF THE
PLATYPUS

find
mate

nurse

4 months

2 years

leave mother

The Peculiar Platypus

1. You can tell that the platypus cannot

    a. fly.   b. swim.   c. dig.

2. What do young platypuses share with all other mammal babies?

    a. They hatch from eggs.   c. They drink their mother's milk.

    b. They can swim.

3. What makes platypuses different from most other mammals?

    a. They live in Australia.   b. They lay eggs.   c. They are small.

4. It takes more than two weeks for platypus eggs to hatch. True or False? Explain.

_____

_____

_____

5. At what age does a platypus first look for a mate?

_____

_____

_____

6. Do you agree with the law that says no one can hunt platypuses? Why or why not?

_____

_____

_____

_____

Kelp: The Underwater Forest

Kelp is an underwater plant. It grows best in cool, shallow seawater that never gets above 70°F. The water must be clear, too. This lets the kelp do photosynthesis*. Kelp is one of the fastest growing plants. With the right conditions, it can grow two feet a day! Kelp is an algae. But it has a root-like structure called a holdfast. This keeps it attached to a rocky surface even during sea storms.

The largest type is called giant kelp. It can have hundreds of branches. Each branch has hundreds of long, narrow leaves. Giant kelp can live for six years and grow up to 200 feet long. In places where kelp grows, the plants form underwater "forests." Many of these forests are found in the Pacific Ocean. Some extend all the way to the Arctic Ocean. They are in the Atlantic Ocean, too. Like rain forests, kelp forests have layers: a canopy, a dimly lit middle, and a dark floor. Different animals live in each of these zones. Many of these creatures eat kelp. In fact, it is the sole diet for some rockfish, sea snails, and urchins. Others, like lobsters and herring, hide below its branches.

People have found lots of uses for kelp. In 1927, the Japanese brought kelp to China. It spread up the coast. Now there are kelp "sea farms." The sea farmers cut just the leaves. Then the plant grows new ones. It takes two or three months. So it's not like cutting a tree. It's more like trimming the grass. Once the kelp is harvested and dried, it is used in fertilizer, animal feed, and health supplements. Kelp has minerals and vitamins. It provides the iodine that's added to our table salt. It keeps the human thyroid gland working right.

Kelp also provides algin. This thickening agent is used in ice cream, salad dressing, and soups. Algin is used in paper, tires, toothpaste, and makeup, too.

Kelp may soon have another use. Scientists say it can be turned into fuel. It can be used to make clean-burning methane. How? First kelp leaves will be cut. Then they will be put into tanks with bacteria. The tanks will be sealed. Without oxygen, the bacteria will break down the kelp. This will make methane. This fuel could replace gasoline.

*a process in which a plant's leaves use sunlight, air, water, and nutrients to make its own food

Kelp: The Underwater Forest

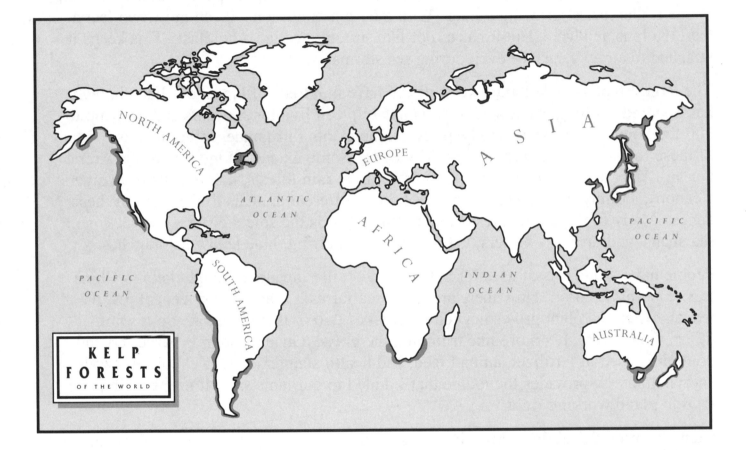

KELP
FORESTS
OF THE WORLD

20

Kelp: The Underwater Forest

1. Kelp contains a mineral that our thyroid glands need called

   a. algin.   b. methane.   c. iodine.

2. Kelp sea farms are located in

   a. Asia.   b. Antarctica.   c. Europe.

3. Kelp stays in one location through the use of a

   a. canopy.   b. holdfast.   c. supplement.

4. A part of kelp is used in making tires and ice cream. True or False? Explain.

_____

_____

_____

5. Look at the map showing where kelp forests thrive. Which continent does not have any kelp growing along its shores? The growing conditions for it are not right there. What conditions do kelp plants need?

_____

_____

_____

_____

6. Will methane made from kelp someday replace gasoline? Why or why not?

_____

_____

_____

_____

Cheetahs Are Fast Cats

Cheetahs are fast cats. They can outrun any other land animal on Earth. They can go from standing still to running 45 miles per hour in just 2.5 seconds. And they can keep up this pace for more than three miles! Their top speed is 70 miles per hour. But they can only go that fast for 300 yards. Cheetahs have a flexible spine that acts as a spring for the back legs. This gives the big cat extra distance between each step. While running, just one foot touches the ground at a time.

The name cheetah means "spotted one." Cheetahs have spots over nearly their whole bodies. Just their white necks and bellies have none. Not only are these big cats beautiful, they will not attack a human. Royalty in ancient cultures often kept them as pets. Paintings show them living with people 5,000 years ago. Although they are easy to tame, today it is against the law to keep one as a pet.

Cheetahs live on grassy plains. They like to lie on tree branches and watch for prey. They do this in the early morning and late afternoon. They hunt rabbits or small antelope.

Each female gives birth to two to eight cubs. But nine out of every 10 cubs die by the age of three months. Lions and hyenas eat them. So, while they are babies, their mother moves them to a new hiding spot each day. By the time they are five months old, the cubs can outrun predators. Babies stay with their mothers for up to two years before finding their own territory.

At one point long ago, nearly all cheetahs died out. Just a few were left to breed. As a result, all cheetahs have similar genes. Now these big cats are dying out again. In 1900 there were 100,000 in Africa and India. Today there are less than 13,000 in Africa. None live in India. Why? People have built homes and farms. This has cut down on the cheetah's hunting grounds. And even though people want to breed them, it hasn't worked well. Cheetahs in zoos rarely breed. Most often if a zoo has a cheetah, it came from the wild.

Cheetahs Are Fast Cats

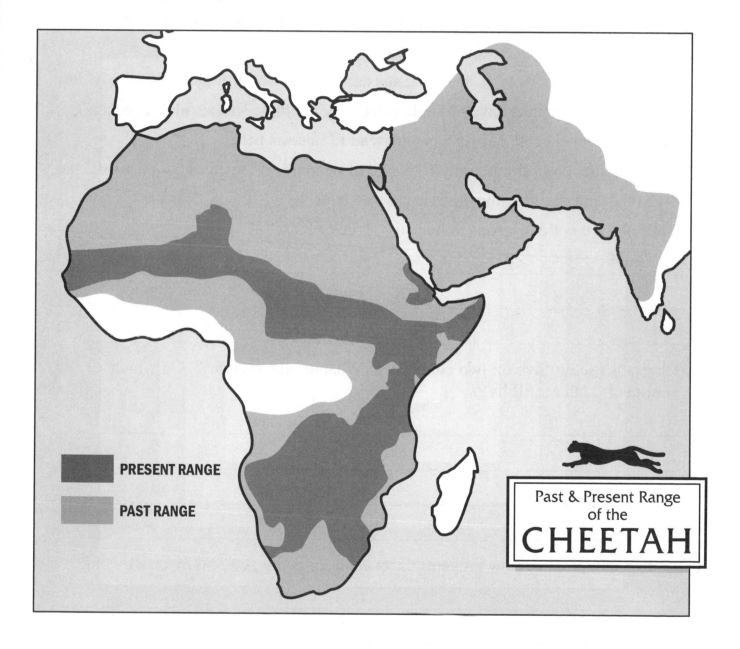

PRESENT RANGE

PAST RANGE

Past & Present Range of the
CHEETAH

Cheetahs Are Fast Cats

1. For a short distance a cheetah can run

    a. 45 miles per hour.   b. 70 miles per hour.   c. 300 miles per hour.

2. Cheetahs hunt

    a. in the afternoon.   b. just after sunset.   c. after it gets completely dark.

3. Since female cheetahs have multiple cubs, why are there so few adult cheetahs?

    a. People steal cheetah babies from the wild to raise as pets.

    b. The mother cheetah will only take care of two cubs no matter how many she has.

    c. Hyenas and lions eat most of the cheetah babies.

4. Cheetahs are not dangerous to humans. True or False? Explain.

_____

_____

_____

5. Cheetahs used to live on two continents. What are their names? On which continent do they still live?

_____

_____

_____

6. Is it good that a law now prevents cheetahs from being pets? Why or why not?

_____

_____

_____

_____

Poisonous Plants: Good or Bad?

Did you know that what tastes good to some species can kill others? Most people like chocolate. It comes from the beans of the cacao tree. But eating even a tiny piece of chocolate can kill a dog! Sometimes just parts of a plant are poisonous, such as the pits of peaches and cherries. So are the green parts of potato and tomato plants.

It's best to never put anything in your mouth unless you know that it is safe. Some flowering shrubs would kill you if you ate any part of them. These include azaleas and rhododendrons.

Tobacco plants' leaves are toxic. Yet they are used in cigarettes. That's why smoking them is bad for the lungs. Chewing tobacco is bad, too. Both can make you ill.

But poisonous plants aren't all bad. The deadliest plant on Earth is the rosary pea. Eating just one will kill you. So people have found another use for them. They use the pretty seeds in jewelry. The berries of deadly nightshade are toxic. Yet the oil from them can save a person who eats a deadly mushroom.

In fact, many medicines come from such plants. They are given in small doses. Digitalis comes from the leaves of foxglove. It has saved the lives of many people with heart trouble. Quinine comes from a rain forest tree. It cures malaria. Mosquitoes spread this deadly disease.

foxglove plant

Poisonous Plants: Good or Bad?

Poisonous Cousins

One you can eat . . . the other you should avoid!

Cashews grow on trees in warm, tropical places. They bear a fruit that people can eat. And at the end of the fruit is a nut. But you cannot just pick these nuts and eat them.

You may have seen cashews in the store. Maybe you've eaten them. These nuts are expensive. Why? They are hard to harvest. Cashews are related to poison ivy. The brown oil between their outer and inner shells causes blisters on human skin. So the nuts must be roasted. This makes the outer shells burst open. The poisonous oil evaporates. The fumes can cause eye and skin irritation.

Poison ivy may be called a pretty plant. But that's the only good thing you can say about it. If you brush against it, it causes a rash on your skin. This rash itches badly. And when you scratch it, the rash spreads!

Getting rid of poison ivy from your yard isn't easy. If you pull it up, you must get the roots. And sometimes you can get the rash even through clothing and gloves. But never set poison ivy on fire! If you inhale the smoke from the fire, you can get poison ivy of the lungs. Only one drug can cure it. And it requires a six-week hospital stay.

Poisonous Plants: Good or Bad?

1. Which part of a tomato plant would be dangerous to eat?

   a. the leaves   b. the tomato   c. the seeds

2. What part of a tobacco plant is poisonous?

   a. roots   b. leaves   c. flowers

3. Which plant has a substance that helps people with heart problems?

   a. foxglove   b. azalea   c. deadly nightshade

4. Every part of the cashew plant is poisonous. True or False? Explain.

_____

_____

_____

5. Is it more dangerous to breathe the smoke of roasting cashews or burning poison ivy? What makes it worse?

_____

_____

_____

6. Should beautiful poisonous plants like rhododendrons be planted in public parks? Tell why or why not.

_____

_____

_____

_____

Around the World in 72 Days

Nellie Bly was the first female reporter. She was born in 1864. At 18, Nellie wrote to the editor of the *Pittsburgh Dispatch*. The newspaper had written a piece that said women are weak. Nellie pointed out how it was wrong. The editor liked her letter. He asked to meet her. He hired her on the spot.

At first she wrote about fashion and cooking. But she wanted to write exciting stories. So in September 1887, Nellie joined the staff of the *New York World*.

Years before, a French man had written a famous novel. It had a character who went around the world in 80 days. At that time it took months to go around the world. No one thought that it could really be done in 80 days. Nellie thought, "I will prove that women are strong. I will go around the world in 75 days!" She had to get the business manager's approval. He said no because she was a woman. Nellie replied, "Very well. Start your man. I'll start the same day for some other newspaper and beat him." The manager knew that she meant it. So he said that she could go.

Nellie wrote a piece saying what she would do. People got excited. Along the way she sent in reports. They told where she was and what was happening. The newspapers sold better than ever before. All over the world people followed her trip. They called her a heroine.

During her trip, Nellie went by steamship, ferry, and rail. At times she had to go without sleep for days in order to make her connections. She adopted a pet monkey. And she faced dangers, including dangerous heat, two bad storms at sea, and a man who wanted to toss her overboard. Just as she reached America's West Coast, the worst snowstorm in 10 years hit. The *New York World* hired a train to take her around the storm. It was a much longer route. But it kept her moving.

Courtesy of the Library of Congress, "Nellie Bly," LC-USZ62-75620

Nellie had left New Jersey on November 14, 1889. She returned on January 25, 1890. Her tour took 72 days, 6 hours, and 11 minutes. Nellie had shown that women are not weak. She wrote a book about her adventures in 1890. Its title? *Around the World in Seventy-two Days*.

Around the World in 72 Days

Nellie Bly Timeline

May 5, 1864	Born Elizabeth Jane Cochran in Pennsylvania
Jan. 1885	Becomes the first U.S. female full-time reporter. Adopts pen name Nellie Bly.
1886	Lives in Mexico and sends back news stories to the *Pittsburgh Dispatch*.
1887	Moves to New York City to write for the *New York World*. Goes undercover into an insane asylum and writes about the bad conditions she finds there.
1888	Goes undercover to write about her experiences at an employment agency, working in a box-making factory, and dancing in a chorus line.
Nov. 1889–Jan. 1890	Travels around the world in record-breaking time.
1895	Marries millionaire Robert Seaman and stops working.
1904	Robert Seaman dies.
1914	Goes to Austria as the first female war reporter covering World War I.
1919	Returns to New York City to write for the *New York Journal*.
Jan. 27, 1922	Dies of pneumonia in New York City.

Around the World in 72 Days

1. Nellie Bly started to write for the *New York World* in

   a. 1887. b. 1889. c. 1890.

2. You can tell that Nellie's business manager at the *New York World* thought that women

   a. were equal to men. c. should be men's servants.

   b. were not equal to men.

3. Nellie's trip around the world took her

   a. more days than she had thought it would.

   b. fewer days than she had thought it would.

   c. exactly the number of days that she had thought it would.

4. While she worked as a reporter, Nellie spent time living in foreign nations. True or False? Explain.

   _____

   _____

   _____

5. List two times that Nellie went undercover to write about a story. Include when each occurred.

   _____

   _____

   _____

   _____

6. Would you enjoy being a newspaper reporter? Why or why not?

   _____

   _____

   _____

   _____

The Search for the Northwest Passage

To sail from the Atlantic Ocean to the Pacific Ocean meant a long trip in 1900. A ship had to go down to the tip of South America. There it would sail through the Strait of Magellan or around Cape Horn. Many sailors hoped that there was another way through the Arctic Ocean. For 400 years, men tried to find a Northwest Passage. Some returned frustrated. Others never came back.

The worst disaster occurred on Sir John Franklin's trip. He took a ship with 129 crew to the area in 1845. They all died. Their ship got trapped in ice near King William Island. The ice did not melt for three years! This was very rare. One good thing came from this tragedy. The search parties sent to look for the men made good maps of the area.

Then, in 1903, Roald Amundsen and seven men started out on *Gjöa*. It was an old fishing boat. It had a square stern (rear). Its hull did not go down very far into the water. Amundsen said that the smaller ship would be easier to steer than a large ship. A square stern would be less likely to get trapped in ice. And he thought that there would be places where the water wasn't very deep. He was right about all these things.

Amundsen sailed from the Atlantic Ocean into the Arctic Ocean. Along the way, he met a group of Inuit. He lived with them for about two years. They taught him the Arctic survival skills he wanted to know. Amundsen took on their lifestyle and wore fur clothes. Once he left the tribe, he finished his trip in just two weeks. In August 1905, he reached the Pacific Ocean. Thick ice was already forming. So he stopped for the winter. The nearest telegraph was 500 miles away in Eagle City, Alaska. Amundsen went by land to get there. On December 5, 1905, he sent a message to tell the world about his success.

Amundsen had sailed and mapped the Northwest Passage. But it was not a useful route. Ice clogged it for most of the year. And it was too hard to go from the west to the east. In fact, that wasn't done until 1942.

Courtesy of the Library of Congress, "Deck of Capt. Amundsen's ship "GJÖA," Nome, Sep. 1st, 1906," LC-USZ62-122067

The Search for the Northwest Passage

Roald Amundsen's Chart of the Northwest Passage

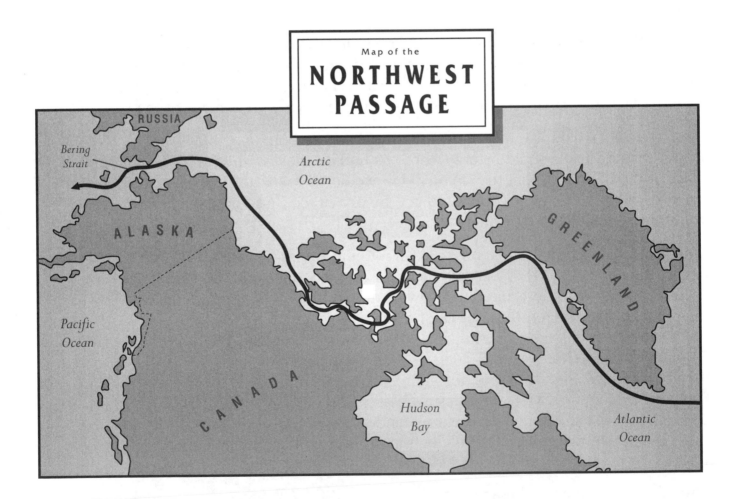

The Search for the Northwest Passage

1. A tragedy occurred in the Northwest Passage expedition that began in

    a. 1845.   b. 1903.   c. 1905.

2. What made Amundsen successful when all others had failed?

    a. He had the biggest ship.   c. He planned ahead and thought
                                      of ways to overcome problems.
    b. He spent more money than
        any other expedition did.

3. How much time passed between when Amundsen completed his journey and when he notified the rest of the world?

    a. one month.   b. more than three months.   c. a year.

4. The Northwest Passage was not an important discovery. True or False? Explain.

_____

_____

_____

5. What is the name of the strait through which Amundsen sailed as part of the Northwest Passage? Name the lands that this strait separates.

_____

_____

_____

_____

6. Should Amundsen have been rewarded with a cash prize for finding the Northwest Passage? Why or why not? _____

_____

_____

_____

The Great Race of Mercy

In January 1925 an outbreak of diphtheria struck Nome, Alaska. It spread fast. There was a cure. But the closest supply of the serum (medicine) was more than 1,000 miles away in Anchorage, Alaska. The only way to save the town's 1,400 people was to get them the medicine quickly. But how?

The serum could travel the first 400 miles by train. It could not go the rest of the way by boat. Ice blocked all the waterways. It could not go by plane, either. Planes had just been invented 20 years before. Pilots could only fly in the summer. There was just one way for the serum to move beyond that point. Sled dogs would carry it.

Twenty teams of 160 dogs shared the trek. They raced around the clock. They braved deadly temperatures. They faced blinding snowstorms and icy winds. They crossed thin ice that had cracks. It took five and a half days to go 674 miles. This was amazing. It was supposed to take at least two weeks.

On January 26, a doctor put the glass bottles of serum into a box. He put the box on the train. Just before midnight on January 27, the first musher (sled driver) and dog team met the train. They began the race across the snowy wilderness. The air was so cold that it could hurt the dogs' lungs. Two of the dogs in the race died this way. The serum had to be kept from freezing. At each stop, it was warmed by wood stoves before the next team left.

The dog teams averaged 6 to 7 miles an hour in brutal cold and darkness. During winter in Alaska, the sun only shines for a few hours at midday. As the dogs approached Nome, a gust of wind flipped the sled on top of the musher! The box tumbled into the blowing snow. The musher took off his gloves and felt through the snow. He found the unbroken bottles. But his fingers never fully recovered from the frostbite caused by this search.

The serum reached Nome on February 2 at 5:30 A.M. It was frozen, but the doctor gave people the shots. The shots worked. The dog sled teams had prevented a disaster. Less than a dozen people died.

Since 1973 the Iditarod Trail Sled Dog Race has been run each year in March. It honors the dogs and mushers who carried the life-saving serum to Nome.

Courtesy of the Library of Congress, "Dog sled arriving from Iditarod," LC-USZ62-131749

The Great Race of Mercy

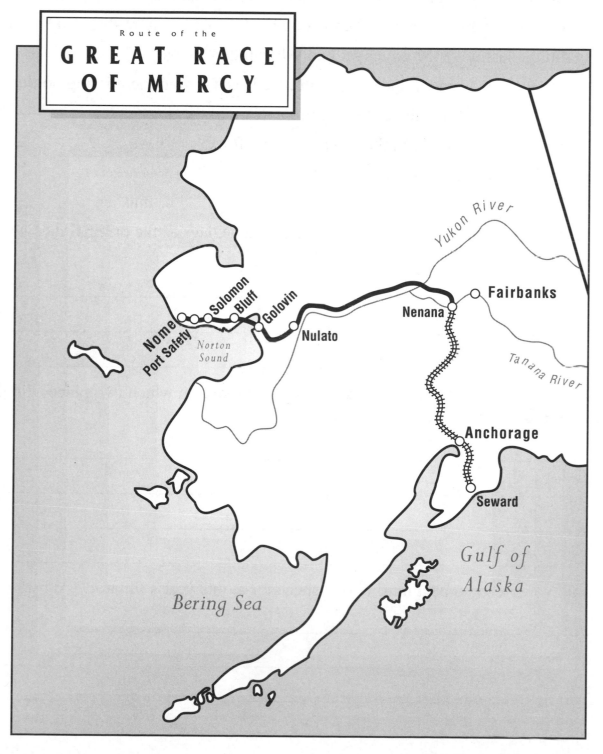

Route of the
**GREAT RACE
OF MERCY**

The Great Race of Mercy

1. How far away from Nome was the medicine before it started on its journey?

   a. more than 400 miles   b. more than 600 miles   c. more than 1,000 miles

2. Why did the last dog sled driver get badly frostbitten hands?

   a. He had to feel around in the snow with bare hands to find the missing bottles.

   b. He had to take off his gloves to take proper care of the dogs.

   c. When his sled fell through the ice, his fingers froze.

3. The people in Nome needed

   a. diphtheria.   b. serum.   c. musher.

4. The Iditarod race is held each year during the same days as the original race was run. True or False? Explain.

_____

_____

_____

5. Look at the map of the route the dog sled teams took. In which two places did they have to cross frozen water?

_____

_____

_____

_____

6. Would you prefer to be a musher or a spectator at this year's Iditarod? Why?

_____

_____

_____

_____

Daring Rescue During the Buffalo Blizzard of 1977

Blizzards are bad snowstorms. They have high winds and cold temperatures. The blowing snow makes it hard to see even a few feet ahead. And the cold can cause frostbite and death. On January 28, 1977, the U.S. Weather Service said that a blizzard would hit Rochester, New York. Children were sent home from school. Factories closed down. Everyone there went home. But the storm missed Rochester. Instead it hit the city of Buffalo 90 miles away.

The people of Buffalo, New York, were used to lots of snow. They live between two Great Lakes. Snow forms over Lake Erie and Lake Ontario. Winds bring the snow to the land. The city of Buffalo gets it from both directions. There was already more than 3 feet of snow on the ground in Buffalo. Another foot of snow fell. Bitter winds of 70 miles per hour whipped it into drifts. The high winds and low temperatures could freeze human skin in less than one minute.

More than 17,000 people were stranded at their jobs. Drivers got stuck in drifts. Most of them got out of their cars and stumbled to shelter. But nine people were stuck above the city. They were on an elevated highway called the Skyway. They set off flares in hopes that someone would see them. Someone saw a flare at 9:30 P.M. and called the police.

Police Chief Larry Ramunno and two other officers put on snowsuits. They walked four blocks to an entrance ramp. Ice formed on their eyebrows. The air was so cold that it hurt to breathe. They were chilled before they even started out onto the highway. The winds could blow them off. So they tied themselves together with a rope. That way if one blew off, the others could pull him up. They brought extra ropes, too.

It took a long time to blaze a path through the deep, swirling snow. At last they reached the cars. The people huddled in them were shivering and in shock. Each officer tied three people to himself. Then they pushed, pulled, and dragged the people to the police station. They could not get to a hospital. So they warmed the people with hot drinks and blankets. Not only did all of the people live, they did not lose any limbs to frostbite.

Daring Rescue During the Buffalo Blizzard of 1977

Fast Facts About the Buffalo Blizzard

❋ Blizzard conditions lasted for 25 hours; the storm itself lasted nearly 72 hours from January 28 through January 31.

❋ Twelve inches of new snow fell.

❋ Temperatures were near 0°F.

❋ Winds gusted up to 70 miles per hour; sustained winds were over 50 miles per hour.

❋ Wind chills reached 60°F below zero.

❋ Snowdrifts were up to 30 feet tall—the height of a three-story building!

❋ Twenty-nine people died, some of them trapped inside their cars.

❋ At the Buffalo Zoo, drifts let three reindeer step over their fence and wander around the city!

❋ Due to the extreme cold, more than 20 animals died at the Buffalo Zoo.

❋ Snow removal lasted for the whole month of February.

Great Adventures and Rescues

Daring Rescue During the Buffalo Blizzard of 1977

1. In Buffalo, the Skyway is a(n)

   a. skyscraper.   b. tall bridge.   c. elevated highway.

2. The part of the blizzard most dangerous to living things was the

   a. amount of snow that fell.   b. wind gusts.   c. extreme cold.

3. How many members of the Buffalo police force helped in the Skyway rescue?

   a. 2   b. 3   c. 9

4. The blizzard caused problems at the Buffalo Zoo. True or False? Explain.

_____

_____

_____

5. How long did it take to remove all the snow from the city of Buffalo?

_____

_____

_____

6. The Carnegie Medal for Bravery is given to those who risk their lives to save others. Should Larry Ramunno and his officers have received the Carnegie Medal for Bravery? Why or why not?

_____

_____

_____

_____

©Teacher Created Resources, Inc.   39   #8373 Document-Based Questions

Stranded Near a Mountaintop

In November 1982 Mark Inglis and Phil Doole joined the search-and-rescue team of Mount Cook National Park. Both men were mountain climbers. They wanted to work on New Zealand's tallest peak. They decided to get to know the 12,315-foot mountain by climbing it.

The pair chose to "climb light." They did not bring a radio, extra clothes, tents, or food. Near the peak a blinding snowstorm with high winds trapped them. They crawled into what they thought was a cave. It turned out to be a tunnel. Icy winds blew through it.

The men needed water. They filled their empty water bottles with snow and melted it against their skin. But this drained their body heat. They shared two candy bars. They huddled together to wait out the storm.

After three days the storm let up enough so that a helicopter could check a hut on the mountain. It was empty. People thought that Mark and Phil had died. But the search leader would not give up. Yet a new storm kept them from doing any more.

After being trapped for a week, the men heard a helicopter. They crawled out of the tunnel and waved. Rescuers dropped them food, water, sleeping bags, and a small grill. Now they had supplies. But they were too weak to climb down.

A team began to climb to the men, but another storm struck! They set up a camp about 3,000 feet below the peak. The moment the storm broke, the team leader sent up a helicopter. It had a rope hanging down. At the end was a rescuer. When the man reached the climbers, he strapped himself to Mark and carried him to camp. They did this again to save Phil. The pair had been stuck near the peak for two weeks.

Both Mark and Phil had frostbite on their legs. They had to have their legs removed below the knee. But both men still climb mountains using artificial legs. And on May 15, 2006, Mark became the first double amputee* to ever reach the peak of Mount Everest. It is the tallest mountain on Earth.

*a person who has had a limb removed

Stranded Near a Mountaintop

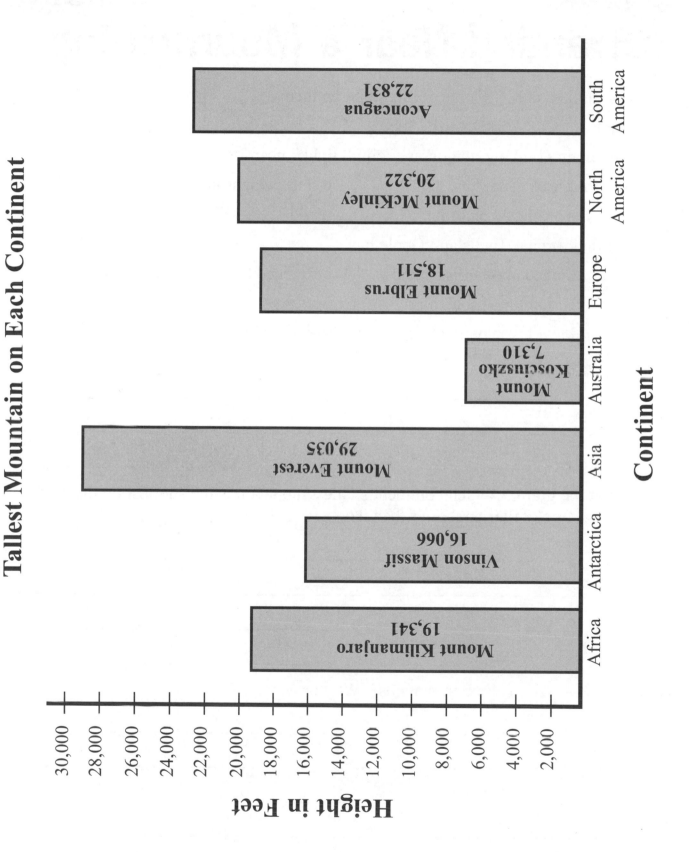

Stranded Near a Mountaintop

1. Mark Inglis and Phil Doole got frostbite on their

    a. hands.   b. legs.   c. ears.

2. In mountain climbing, the phrase "climb light" means to

    a. not bring extra supplies.   c. lose weight in order to be
                                         able to climb faster.

    b. wear light-colored clothing.

3. Since their ordeal, Inglis and Doole have

    a. never climbed another mountain.   c. learned how to fly helicopters.

    b. continued to climb mountains.

4. The world's tallest mountain lies on the continent of South America. True or False?
Explain.

_____

_____

_____

5. Look at the graph. Which continent's tallest mountain is the shortest on the chart?
Is Mount Cook taller or shorter than it?

_____

_____

_____

_____

6. Would you like to climb mountains? Why or why not?

_____

_____

_____

_____

A Monster Wave Flips Two Boats

The Vendee Globe Race is a sailboat race around the world. Each sailor is alone. Each one tries to use the wind and sea currents to go the fastest. But there is great danger in sailing alone in the stormy Southern Ocean. This sea surrounds Antarctica. It often has deadly storms.

On January 9, 1997, Tony Bullimore and Theirry Dubois were on boats in this sea. Suddenly a monster wave as tall as a 10-story building struck Tony's *Exide Challenger*. The boat flipped over and lost its keel. The keel is the fin on the boat's bottom that keeps it upright. Tony was trapped inside the cabin under the water. He put on a survival suit to stay warm in the cold water. But he did not have the hood, gloves, or boots. So his head, hands, and feet grew numb.

Tony climbed onto a counter. He found two candy bars and ate them slowly. But he needed water more than food. Luckily his desalination pump still worked. He put seawater into it. Fresh water came out. It took 1,000 pumps with his numb hands to get one cup of water.

The huge wave continued on for miles and capsized Theirry's boat as well. He climbed onto his overturned boat to get out of the water. Both boats had distress beacons that turned on when the boats overturned. Rescue was on the way. A search plane found Theirry first. It dropped him a lifeboat filled with supplies. Then it went to look for Tony. A storm stopped the air search. Instead an Australian navy ship headed toward Tony's position.

For four days Tony had crouched on a ledge near icy cold water. His boat was sinking, and he was running out of time. Suddenly he heard a motor. He swam out through a broken window. He splashed about wildly in the waves. An inflatable speedboat had been lowered from the navy ship. It rushed toward him. He was saved!

Frostbite scarred his feet and face. But Tony was lucky. He did not lose any body parts. He still loves to race. But now he has a watertight box packed with survival gear. He's not taking any more chances.

A Monster Wave Flips Two Boats

You know that the ocean's water is salty. But did you know that drinking salt water can kill you? The human body cannot stand too much salt. The body's cells give off water in order to dilute the saltiness of the seawater. As the cells lose water, the body dehydrates. The person dies.

But seawater can be made safe to drink. It can be changed into fresh water through a desalination pump, like this one:

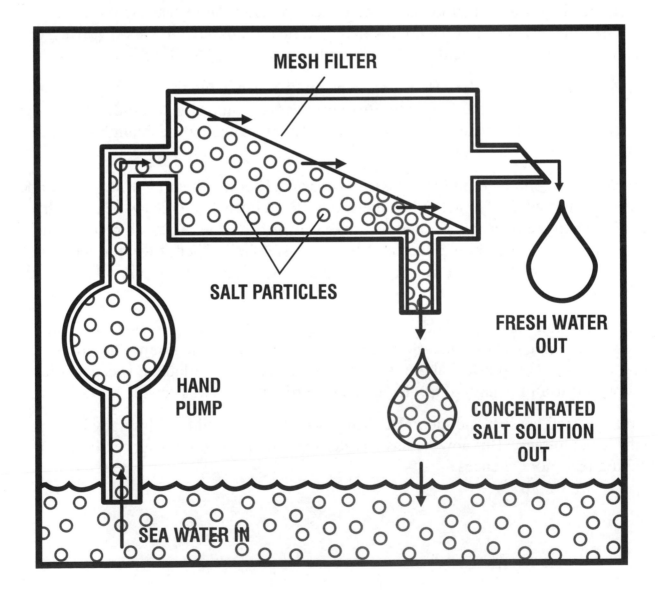

A Monster Wave Flips Two Boats

1. Who found the *Exide Challenger*?

   a. Theirry Dubois   b. a search plane   c. an Australian naval ship

2. The towering monster wave was

   a. able to travel for many miles.   c. moving in a gigantic circle.

   b. a freak event in just one spot.

3. The word *capsized* means

   a. rescued.   b. sent out a distress signal.   c. overturned.

4. The monster wave occurred in the ocean that surrounds the continent of Australia. True or False? Explain.

_____

_____

_____

5. Look at the diagram of the desalination pump. What part of it traps the salt particles?

_____

_____

_____

6. For safety's sake, should a desalination pump be required on every ocean-going ship and boat? Why or why not?

_____

_____

_____

Trapped Underground!

In July 2002 coal miners worked underground in the Quecreek Coal Mine near Pittsburgh, Pennsylvania. Their shaft was 12 feet wide but just four feet high. Nine men ran the mechanical miner. This machine drilled into the seam of coal. Chunks of coal moved down a conveyor belt to railroad cars.

Suddenly water gushed into the mine shaft. The nine men ran downhill toward the elevator. It could take them to the surface. But the water got there first. The men turned and, breathing in a tiny space near the ceiling, they walked back on the conveyor belt.

The mine's owners rushed to the scene. They knew that the men were under a field. But where? They had to drill a hole to get air to the miners. They looked at a map of the mine's shafts. If the men were still alive, they would go to the highest ground. The owners found the coordinates of the highest shaft. Then they used GPS* to find the right spot in the field. Pumps began removing 20,000 gallons of water per minute.

While the men above worked to drill a hole, the men below worked to hold back the water. They used cement blocks to build a wall. But the water surged over the top of it. They retreated to a higher spot. At last the drill bit from above broke through near them. The men hit the pipe nine times to tell that they were alive. But rising water soon buried the pipe bringing them air. The men squeezed together in the only dry spot. Air from above was forced down the pipe. It bubbled through the water and gave the men air (like air blown down a straw into a drink).

Now the men above were drilling a bigger hole so that they could lower a rescue cage. But their drill broke! It took many hours to get the old drill bit out of the ground and bring in a new one. They had to start a new hole. At last, more than three days after the accident, the rescue crew broke into the mineshaft.

The men had been in total darkness. They had shut off their headlamps to save the power. Just two lamps still worked. They switched them on. In the dim light, they saw a welcome sight. A rescue cage had been lowered to them. One by one, each man got into the cage. A cheering crowd on the surface met each man. Loved ones ran to hug the men.

Only one of the miners kept his job. The rest refused to go back into the coal mine.

*Global positioning system—a system in which three satellites pinpoint an exact location on Earth's surface and send the information to a receiver

Trapped Underground!

The Global Positioning System (GPS) helped to save the miners' lives. It let the people above know where to drill.

The U.S. Air Force has 24 GPS satellites in space. Each one has a set orbit. Each stays a constant distance from Earth. Each one sends out signals all the time. The spot where three of these signals meet tells where a place lies on Earth's surface. It is correct to within 33 feet. The location is shown on a GPS receiver.

How GPS Works

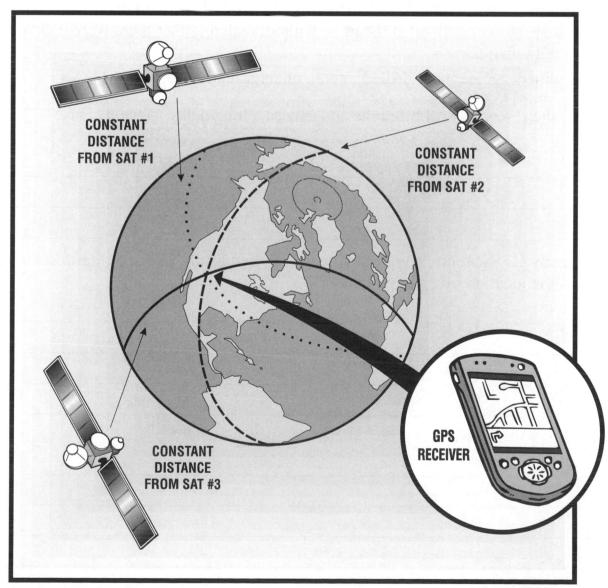

Trapped Underground!

1. How long after the accident happened did it take to rescue the trapped miners?

   a. 2 days   b. 3 days   c. 5 days

2. A mechanical miner is

   a. part of the GPS system.   c. a machine.

   b. a piece of equipment used
      to rescue the men.

3. What caused the mine to flood?

   a. The miners flooded the mine on purpose to protest their low pay.

   b. The mine's owners flooded the mine without realizing that there were people working down there.

   c. The miners accidentally drilled into an underground water supply.

4. During the rescue, a drill bit broke and caused a long delay. True or False? Explain.

_____

_____

_____

5. How many GPS satellite signals are needed to find a single spot on Earth's surface? How is the location given to people?

_____

_____

_____

_____

6. Would you like to work in a coal mine? Why or why not?

_____

_____

_____

_____

Krakatau, a Deadly Volcano

After years of silence, a volcano awoke in May 1883. Ash and smoke came from its cone. For three months it shook and rumbled. But the volcano had not actually erupted for over 200 years. No one could have guessed what would happen next.

Krakatau stood on a small island in the Indian Ocean. It had formed over millions of years. Lava flowed up from the sea floor. At last the volcano stood 2,700 feet high. No one lived on the island with the volcano. But thousands of people made their homes 40 miles away. They lived on the islands of Sumatra and Java. When they first felt the earth shake and saw the clouds of smoke and dust, some of them moved to higher ground. But they couldn't stay there long. They had to go back to their farms and homes.

On August 27 at 5:30 A.M. Krakatau erupted. It made so much noise that it woke up people thousands of miles away. A second blast occurred an hour later. But Krakatau wasn't done. Shortly after 10 A.M. the island blew up with more force than 1,000 atom bombs. Two-thirds of the land shot into the air. It formed a huge cloud.

The rest of the land fell into the center. This caused another big blast. Seawater poured into the deep new crater. So much water was displaced that a 100-foot-high tsunami went racing toward Java and Sumatra. No one knew the tall wave was coming. They had no time to flee. It wiped out hundreds of villages. More than 36,000 people died.

Some people were 30 miles away on the ship *Charles Bal*. The black clouds blocked the sun. The captain told everyone to go below deck. Then he took down the sails to keep them from being ripped to shreds. Strong winds carried the volcanic ash over the sea. The ship was caked with a thick, cement-like layer of ash and mud. Yet the big wave did not crash over it. It went right under the boat. So those people lived to tell their tale.

Krakatau, a Deadly Volcano

On the morning of August 27, 1883, a telegram was sent from Batavia to Singapore. It stated:

> AT DAYBREAK TERRIFIC DETONATIONS[1] FROM KRAKATAU HEARD AS FAR AS SOERAKARTA. ASHES FALLING AS FAR AS CHERIBON. FLASHES PLAINLY VISIBLE FROM HERE.

[1]explosions

A second telegram arrived at noon:

> SERANG IN TOTAL DARKNESS. STONES FALLING. VILLAGE NEAR ANJER WASHED AWAY. BATAVIA NOW QUITE DARK. UNABLE TO COMMUNICATE WITH ANJER. FEAR CALAMITY[2] THERE. . . . BELIEVE ALL LOST.

[2]disaster

On the morning of August 28, Singapore received this message:

> ANJER, TJERINGIN, AND TELOK BETONG DESTROYED. WHERE ONCE MOUNT KRAKATAU STOOD, THE SEA NOW PLAYS.

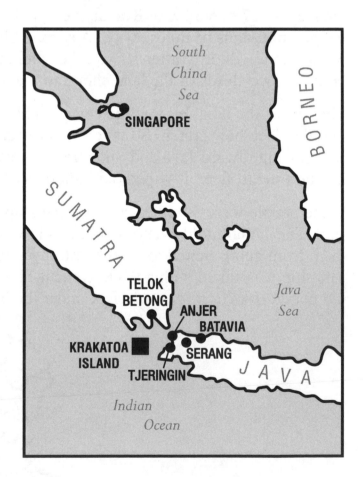

Krakatau, a Deadly Volcano

1. Most of the people who died were on

a. islands near Krakatau.   c. the island of Krakatau.

b. the ship *Charles Bal*.

2. The most deadly part of Krakatau's eruption was the

a. clouds of volcanic ash that made the world's temperature drop for years.

b. hurricane-force winds it generated.

c. tsunami it caused.

3. How much time passed between when Krakatau started rumbling and when it erupted in 1883?

a. one month   b. three months   c. six months

4. The people who died in the disaster never knew that Krakatau had erupted. True or False? Explain.

_____

_____

_____

5. What are Anjer, Tjeringin, and Telok Betong? Where are they located?

_____

_____

_____

_____

6. Should people be allowed to live in areas that have active volcanoes? Why or why not?

_____

_____

_____

_____

Destructive Wind and Water: The Galveston Hurricane

The worst natural disaster in U.S. history occurred more than 100 years ago. It happened in Galveston, Texas, in 1900. A strong hurricane hit the island. More people died in this storm than in all other U.S. hurricanes between 1901 and 2006 added together.

At that time about 38,000 people lived on the island of Galveston. It is really a sandbar[1] just 2 miles wide and 25 miles long. It lies in the Gulf of Mexico, just off the Texas coast.

In early September the U.S. Weather Bureau tracked a hurricane. It started near Cuba. It moved toward Texas. Two of the forecasters got on horses. They went down the streets and beaches. They told the people to get off the island. A man raised two flags on a pole atop the Weather Bureau building. One meant that a bad storm was coming. The other flag told its direction. The people knew what the flags meant. But most of them did not want to leave their homes. By the time they chose to do so, the bridges joining the city to the mainland had washed away. They were stranded on a sandbar with a hurricane bearing down on them.

A hurricane causes a storm surge. A storm surge is like a big wall of water. It hits the shore before the rest of the storm. The storm surge was 20 feet above sea level. And the city was just five feet above sea level. The whole island flooded. Water turned the soil to mud. Some buildings tilted. Others caved in. Coffins came out of their graves and floated in the water.

Then the storm struck. High winds tore off roofs and wrecked buildings. Waves pounded the shore. Docks vanished. Sixteen ships were moored in the harbor. All broke free. They sailed through the city and smashed into things.

The storm killed at least 8,000 people. Once the city recovered, its citizens built a huge stone seawall. They hoped to keep the water from ever again covering their city. Fifteen years later another big hurricane hit Galveston. The seawall worked well. It kept the worst of the waves out of the city.

[1] a ridge of sand built up by waves and currents

Courtesy of the Library of Congress, "Galveston disaster, trying to find where their home stood," LC-USZ62-12022

Destructive Wind and Water: The Galveston Hurricane

This telegram was sent the night after the storm ended:

HOUSTON, TEXAS

11:25 P.M.

SEPTEMBER 9, 1900

TO: WILLIS MOORE

CHIEF, U.S. WEATHER BUREAU

FIRST NEWS FROM GALVESTON JUST RECEIVED BY TRAIN. IT COULD GET NO CLOSER TO THE BAY SHORE THAN SIX MILES WHERE PRAIRIE WAS STREWN WITH DEBRIS[1] AND DEAD BODIES. ABOUT 200 CORPSES COUNTED FROM THE TRAIN. LARGE STEAMSHIP STRANDED TWO MILES INLAND.

NOTHING COULD BE SEEN OF GALVESTON. LOSS OF LIFE AND PROPERTY UNDOUBTEDLY MOST APPALLING.[2] WEATHER CLEAR AND BRIGHT HERE WITH GENTLE SOUTHEAST WIND.

G. L. VAUGHAN

MANAGER, WESTERN UNION, HOUSTON

[1]wreckage

[2]shocking

Destructive Wind and Water: The Galveston Hurricane

1. How many ships sailed into the city during the storm?

   a. 5   b. 16   c. 20

2. What did the people of Galveston do after the terrible hurricane of 1900?

   a. They left the island without rebuilding, realizing it would never be safe.

   b. They built hurricane-proof houses and buildings on the island.

   c. They built a seawall around the island to keep it safe from high water.

3. How much higher than sea level was the storm surge compared to the city of Galveston?

   a. 5 feet   b. 15 feet   c. 20 feet

4. The people of Galveston had some warning that a bad hurricane was coming. True or False? Explain.

_____

_____

_____

5. Name two things that the telegram states were seen from the train.

_____

_____

_____

_____

6. Is it wise for people to live in Galveston today? Why or why not?

_____

_____

_____

_____

The Dust Bowl

During the 1930s over three million people moved from the Great Plains. They left Oklahoma, Texas, New Mexico, and Kansas. They went to California. This was more people than had gone in all of the gold rushes. This was more people than had come in search of free land. In fact, this was the biggest westward migration ever in U.S. history. Why did it happen? The people were fleeing the Dust Bowl.

The first farmers went to the Midwest in the 1800s. They felt lucky to plow and plant just two acres. By the 1920s farmers had better farm equipment. They plowed lots of acres. They were proud of their long, straight rows of crops. They didn't waste any land with rows of trees for windbreaks. Cattle and horses grazed on the prairie. They ate most of the grass that held the dirt in place.

Then, in 1931, a seven-year drought began. No rain fell. Without it, the crops died. When the wind blew across the flat Great Plains, nothing slowed it down. The long dry spell and high winds lifted the dirt into the air. It blew around like snow in a blizzard. These dust storms blew millions of tons of dirt as far east as Washington, D.C.! What had once been rich farmland looked like a desert. The dust storms ruined 50 million acres. They are one of the worst environmental disasters in world history.

The cattle and sheep breathed the dust. Then they died. Many people died from breathing the dust, too. The dust wrecked car and tractor engines. It blew through tiny cracks in homes. So much blew into some attics that the ceilings fell in!

At last the families gave up. They left their farms. They went to the West Coast in search of jobs. But there were not enough jobs in California. The people living there resented the newcomers. They didn't want to compete for jobs. They called the refugees "Okies." Hatred toward them was so bad that some farmers burned their extra crops. They didn't want to share them with the hungry Okies!

The U.S. government tried to help those who stayed in the Dust Bowl. They told the farmers to plant crops in rows that ran across the typical winds. They also planted over 18,500 miles of trees to form windbreaks.

The Dust Bowl

The Resettlement Administration was a U.S. government program set up in 1935 to help farmers in the Dust Bowl. Here is one of the posters from the Resettlement Administration. It was posted in towns throughout the Midwest.

Courtesy of the Library of Congress, "Years of Dust," LC-USZ62-19225

The Dust Bowl

1. How many people left the Dust Bowl and went west?

   a. more than 3 million   b. about 10 million   c. 50 million

2. Why did the people in California refuse to welcome the Okies?

   a. There wasn't enough food for everyone.

   b. There weren't enough jobs for everyone.

   c. There wasn't enough water for everyone.

3. How was the dust dangerous to the health of people and animals?

   a. Breathing too much dust could kill people and animals.

   b. When the dust got into food, it poisoned people and animals.

   c. If the dust got into milk, it was no longer safe to drink.

4. One the factors that caused the Dust Bowl was a lack of trees on farms. True or False? Explain.

_____

_____

_____

5. Look at the poster. What is the look on the farmer's face? Why does he look that way?

_____

_____

_____

_____

6. Did the U.S. government act quickly enough to help farmers in the Dust Bowl?

_____

_____

_____

_____

Avalanche!

An avalanche occurs when a mass of snow breaks free near the top of a mountain. It rushes to the valley below. As it slides, the snow buries everything in its path. It can cover trees, animals, people, and towns. No one knows how often they race down the world's many mountains. Scientists think that each year about one million do! Luckily most of these are small. But when a big avalanche happens, people can die.

Avalanches often occur after heavy snowfall. The snow's weight makes it unstable. Even a loud sound can make it start sliding. It picks up speed and more snow as it roars down the side of the mountain. There's only one thing to do once an avalanche starts: Get out of its way!

An earthquake caused an avalanche in the worst natural disaster to ever hit South America. An earthquake happens when big plates far below the ground slide. They move under or against each other. This makes everything above the ground shake and slide around.

The morning of May 31, 1970, was normal for people in the town of Yungay, Peru. Then, in the afternoon, the animals started to act odd. Flocks of birds took to the air. They would not perch on anything. Cows would not go into their barns. Dogs that weren't tied up ran away. The animals sensed a disaster about to happen. A strong earthquake shook the town. Streets cracked. Buildings fell down. But most of the people survived. Then they heard a rumble. It came from the slopes of the nation's tallest mountain.

The quake had shaken the mountain. Millions of tons of rock, snow, and ice tore loose. It slid down and crashed into lakes. The lakes burst from their banks. A wave of mud, ice, and rocks rushed toward the town at 180 miles per hour. It took just three minutes for it to go 10 miles. No one had time to get away. Tons of ice, mud, and rock buried Yungay. Most of the 20,000 people who lived there died. Just 92 people on the far edge of the town lived.

✚ SKI SAFETY TIPS ✚

Avalanche!

High Ridge Ski Resort Safety Brochure—Avalanche Survival Tips

We want you to be safe. When you are on the mountain, you must wear the rescue beacon given to you at check-in. If you don't, your lift pass will be taken away.

We have people who check the mountain at dawn. They report to a helicopter crew that drops explosives. This causes controlled slides and stops bigger ones. Still, snow sports involve risk. We cannot control nature. So, if an avalanche starts while you're on the mountain, here's what to do:

1. **Get Out of the Way!** Get off the ski run. Move at a right angle to the slide. Get into the trees. Even if the snow overtakes you there, it will be going more

slowly. The trees will also trap much of the snow.

2. **Take Shelter!** Get off the ski run. Get under a rock shelf. Even if the snow buries the shelf, the area under it will have an air pocket. This will let you breathe until rescuers can dig you out.

3. **Abandon Your Equipment!** Your equipment may cause you to twist and break a bone. If you are in the slide, kick off your skis or snowboard. Drop your poles.

4. **Stay on Top of the Snow!** If you're caught in moving snow, use your arms and legs to "swim" to stay on top of the snow. When it stops moving, the closer to the surface you are, the better.

5. **Move Around!** As the snow starts to slow down, move your arms and legs. This will make a small air pocket for you once the slide stops.

6. **Stay Calm!** If you're trapped under the snow and can't move, don't struggle. Stay calm to use your air slowly.

7. **Turn on Your Rescue Beacon!** By following its signal, we can find you fast.

Avalanche!

1. The avalanche that buried Yungay, Peru, started because of a(n)

    a. heavy snowfall.   b. loud noise.   c. earthquake.

2. Most of the world's avalanches

    a. kill thousands of people.   c. are small and may not even be noticed.

    b. bury entire towns.

3. Right before the earthquake, which animals began to act strangely?

    a. dogs   b. snakes   c. fish

4. The earthquake itself caused little damage to Yungay. True or False? Explain.

_____

_____

_____

5. Could the information given in the High Ridge Ski Resort Safety Brochure have saved the lives of the people in the Yungay, Peru, avalanche?

_____

_____

_____

6. Is it fair for High Ridge to take away a person's lift pass (which was paid for) if the person refuses to wear a rescue beacon? Why or why not?

_____

_____

_____

Flash Flood in Big Thompson Canyon

A flash flood occurs when heavy rains fall upstream. Downstream the weather may be fine. But a river or stream can rise fast from all the rainwater running into it. A wall of water gushes down a river or stream in a flash flood. The people downstream may have no warning.

Big Thompson Canyon is in Colorado. It is a part of the Rocky Mountains. The narrow, 25-mile-long gorge has steep rock walls. A road winds through this area. It follows the Big Thompson River. Much of the canyon is narrow. There is just room for the road and the river. Campgrounds and cabins occupy space wherever the gorge widens.

On July 31, 1976, storms upstream made the river's level rise 19 feet. The Colorado State Police and local sheriffs knew this meant trouble. They sent officers into the canyon. They told the people of the danger of a flash flood. Since no rain had fallen in their area, few people paid attention. Some would live to regret that. Others would not be so lucky.

About 6:30 P.M. heavy rain started to fall in the canyon. Soon mud, trees, and rocks slid down the gorge walls. They blocked the road. Cars and trucks could not get around them. Many people were trapped in their cars. When lightning flashed, they saw that the river was almost up to the road. But where could they go?

Some got out of their cars. They climbed up the unstable rock wall. The rocks were slippery and it was dark. A few people found it too hard. They went back to their cars. Soon the water rose so high that their cars started to float down the roaring river.

The high water lasted for three hours. During that time two miles of the road crumbled into the raging rapids. Houses bobbed down the river. So did tractor trailers and big motor homes. People trapped in the water clung to anything they could. The strong current tore off their clothes. All they could do was hang on and hope that nothing big hit them. When the storm died down, helicopters lowered ropes to them. Twenty-five years later, in 2001, a statue was made to honor the 144 people who died.

Everyone knows that one day the gorge will flood again. They hope that the next time, people will heed the warnings. Now signs line the gorge. They state "Climb to Safety."

Flash Flood in Big Thompson Canyon

Great Flash Flood Memorial Plaque

IN MEMORY OF TWO GALLANT
LAW ENFORCEMENT OFFICERS

COLORADO STATE PATROL
SGT. W. HUGH PURDY

ESTES PARK PATROLMAN
MICHEL O. CONLEY

THEY GAVE THEIR LIVES TO SAVE THE LIVES OF OTHERS
THE NIGHT OF JULY 31, 1976 WHEN MORE THAN 140 PERSONS
DIED IN THE GREAT FLASH FLOOD OF BIG THOMPSON CANYON.

"LORD OF HOSTS PROTECT US YET
LEST WE FORGET . . . LEST WE FORGET."

ERECTED BY THE GRATEFUL CITIZENS OF COLORADO
DEDICATED 7-31-78

Flash Flood in Big Thompson Canyon

1. How long is Big Thompson Canyon?

   a. 19 miles long   b. 25 miles long   c. 144 miles long

2. Why didn't the people in the canyon leave after the officers warned them of the danger?

   a. They didn't believe the officers because it hadn't rained in the canyon.

   b. They had no way to leave the canyon.

   c. Most of the people were deaf and couldn't hear the warning.

3. Why have signs been posted along the gorge since the flash flood?

   a. to tell people that it's best to stay in their cars during a flood

   b. to guide people to the flood shelters that have been built

   c. to warn people that they must climb the rock walls during a flood

4. The Big Thompson Canyon Flash Flood plaque was put up two years after the flash flood occurred. True or False? Explain.

_____

_____

_____

5. What were the names of the two officers who died trying to save others from the flash flood in Big Thompson Canyon? How do you know?

_____

_____

_____

_____

6. Should the officers who warned the people to leave the gorge have forced them to go? Why or why not?

_____

_____

_____

_____

Deadly Cloud from Lake Nyos

In Cameroon, Africa, a lake lies above an old volcano. How did it get there? The volcano had a deep crater, or hole. Over time rain filled it with water. The result was Lake Nyos.

The volcano no longer erupts. But gases from it still seep into the lake. Carbon dioxide goes into the deepest waters of the lake. It stays there just as carbon dioxide stays inside an unopened can of soda. Over time the lake built up a lot of carbon dioxide mixed in the water. This water was a bit heavier than normal water. So it didn't rise. The weight of the water above it held it down, too.

But then something happened. In the early morning of August 21, 1986, the carbon dioxide water rose to the top of the lake. Carbon dioxide bubbles formed, just like when you open a can of soda and fizz comes out. These bubbles pulled up more carbon dioxide water. Soon billions of bubbles rushed to the surface. They formed a cloud that burst from the lake. So much gas escaped that the lake's water level dropped three feet!

Carbon dioxide is heavy. It didn't rise into the sky. Instead the cloud swept over the surrounding land. People and animals need oxygen. If there is too much carbon dioxide in the air, they cannot get enough oxygen. The deadly cloud moved over a few towns. About 1,700 sleeping people never woke up. Cows and wildlife died, too.

No one knows why this happened. Some think that there was a landslide. Tons of rock and dirt slid into the lake. This stirred up the water. Others say that there must have been a slight volcanic eruption under the lake. It pushed up the deep water.

Scientists know that other lakes have carbon dioxide in their depths as well. They are in Africa, too. After the Lake Nyos tragedy, people wanted to take action. They did not want a cloud to come from any of these lakes. They had to stop the lake waters from getting gas-charged. So pumps have been put at the bottom of each lake. They bring up the deep water a little at a time. This lets the deep water lose its carbon dioxide slowly. Then a big bubble cannot form. This solution looks good, too. There's a fountain in the middle of each lake.

64

Deadly Cloud from Lake Nyos

Strange Disaster in Cameroon Takes 1,700 Lives

NPI, August 22, 1986—Yesterday in the early morning hours a cloud of carbon dioxide (CO_2) burst from Lake Nyos in Cameroon. The gas cloud quickly spread over two villages. It killed at least 1,700 people and 3,500 head of livestock. About 4,000 people were able to flee. They are being treated for breathing problems.

No one knows what caused this rare and deadly event. Scientists say that a landslide, minor earthquake, or slight volcanic eruption may have triggered the gas release. Lake Nyos fills the crater of extinct volcano Mount Oku. A pocket of magma lies below the lake. It leaks CO_2 into the water. But usually the CO_2 remains in solution in the lowest layer of water.

The clear blue waters of Lake Nyos are now a murky red. This is due to the iron-rich water that rose to the surface with the CO_2. The lake's level dropped from the huge volume of gas released. Trees on the shore were knocked down, too. This means that the outgassing caused an overflow of the lake's waters, like soda overflowing when a can is opened.

Two other lakes are known to have this condition. They are Lake Monoun, also in Cameroon, and Lake Kivu in Rwanda. Scientists from many nations are heading to the area to learn more.

Deadly Cloud from Lake Nyos

1. Lake Nyos lies above a(n)

    a. earthquake fault.   b. old volcano.   c. natural spring.

2. What happened to 1,700 people living near Lake Nyos on August 21, 1986?

    a. They fled from the area and were treated for breathing problems.

    b. They died in their sleep.

    c. They saw all of their cows die.

3. After the cloud came from Lake Nyos, its water looked

    a. the same as before.   b. clear blue.   c. a murky red.

4. Scientists know what caused the deadly cloud to come from Lake Nyos. True or False? Explain.

_____

_____

_____

5. Read the newspaper article. What are the names of the three lakes that have this carbon dioxide problem? What does CO_2 stand for?

_____

_____

_____

6. Are the people living near Lake Nyos today safe? Why or why not?

_____

_____

_____

Gunpowder Inventions

For thousands of years, humans have looked for new ways to win battles. As a result, wars often bring about new inventions.

Around the year 1000, the Chinese made gunpowder. They found that sulfur, saltpeter, charcoal, and pitch exploded if touched by a spark. By 1288 they had cannons. They used gunpowder to fire cannonballs at invaders. Each cannon was made one at a time. No two were alike. The person firing one had to know its quirks in order to aim it. The nations with cannons had an advantage over those that didn't. Cannons changed the course of history.

The first guns looked like small cannons. They were carried over the shoulder and fired just the same way. A gunpowder charge was rammed down the barrel. Then a charge was lit. These guns were heavy and hard to use. It took a lot of time to load, aim, and fire them once. After about 1400, guns that could be carried on a person's body became smaller, more accurate, and more common.

American patriot David Bushnell invented floating mines in 1775. He wanted to cause enough damage to sink an enemy ship. He coated wooden kegs with tar. This kept out water. Then he packed gunpowder in the kegs. Just a light shock would make them explode. If a British ship bumped into one, it would blow a hole in its side.

Removing mines from the ocean after World War I.

In December 1777 Bushnell sent a group of these kegs floating down the Delaware River. He wanted to stop the British ships. They had supplies for their troops in Philadelphia. He hoped their ships would hit the kegs. But all of the kegs got jammed in ice. Two boys saw them. They walked out on the ice to check them out. Both were killed. The tragedy tipped off the British. They found a way to blow up the kegs safely. Their sailors went out and got rid of the rest of them.

Since then water mines have been used in many wars. The newer mines worked because they have been hidden below the water's surface.

Gunpowder Inventions

Julia Chang   Mr. Rodriguez

Language Arts   Report

Fireworks

Gunpowder is used to make fireworks. You've probably seen them. They are set off at night as part of a festival. Fireworks get shot into the sky. Then they blow up. They make colorful sparks and loud noises.

Fireworks start out as hollow cardboard tubes filled with gunpowder. A fuse sticks into this gunpowder. The fuse is a thick cotton string. It's been soaked in saltpeter. When a match lights the fuse, it burns the gunpowder. This makes the rocket shoot into the air. Then the gunpowder lights a smaller packet of gunpowder. This blows up the cardboard tube. It ignites tiny firecrackers at the top of the rocket, too.

Small amounts of chemicals are added to the gunpowder. They make the different colors. When sodium is added, the fireworks are yellow. When copper is added, the fireworks are blue. Charcoal gives the fireworks a sparkling tail.

You should not play with fireworks. They are dangerous. Gunpowder can explode from a small spark. If they blow up near you, you can be hurt or killed. That's why a lot of states won't let stores sell fireworks. That way only experts can set them off.

Fireworks have other uses, too. You may have seen red flares on a road around an accident. They burn for a long time. They do not blow up, but they are a kind of firework. Railroads use big firecrackers called torpedoes. (Firecrackers just make noise.) These torpedoes blow up as a train runs over them. The engineer knows to put on the brakes because there's danger ahead.

Gunpowder Inventions

1. Gunpowder was invented around

   a. 1000.   b. 1288.   c. 1775.

2. The first guns looked most like

   a. fireworks.   b. cannons.   c. mines.

3. Why did David Bushnell invent floating mines?

   a. He wanted to blow up Philadelphia.

   b. He wanted to keep the Chinese from going up the Delaware River.

   c. He wanted to blow up British ships.

4. It is OK for you to set off fireworks without an adult present. True or False? Explain.

5. Name and describe two uses for fireworks.

6. Should people other than police and the military be allowed to own guns? Tell why.

The Miracle of Movable Type

Long ago every book had to be copied by hand using a quill pen. A quill pen was a bird feather dipped in ink. It was hard to use without making ink blots. Monks made books. They spent years making one copy of a book. Once they finished, they started all over again to make another copy. This made books cost so much that only the rich could buy them. With so few books, ideas and knowledge spread slowly.

Johannes Gutenberg worked in Germany's mint making coins. He heated gold or silver and poured the liquid metal into molds. When the metal cooled, it was a coin. Gutenberg had an idea. He wanted to make separate letters out of metal. In 1428 Gutenberg started working in secret on his project. But he needed funds to buy metal and equipment. In 1448 he had to borrow money. About two years later, he printed his first book. It was a 641-page Bible. It was written in Latin. He made about 300 copies. One of these is on display in the Library of Congress in Washington, D.C. Think about how old it is!

How did Gutenberg do it? He had invented movable type, or the printing press. He had made hundreds of pieces of type. He made each letter of the alphabet. Can you guess what letters he made the most pieces of? The vowels *a* and *e*. That's because they are used in so many words. There were also punctuation marks.

He used the letters to form words. He set the words in rows in a tray. Then he rolled ink onto the "type." Next he pressed paper against it. (This is how it got the name *printing press*.) The ink on the type pieces came off on the paper. He hung the page up to dry. Then a person sewed the pages in order using sturdy thread. At last a fabric cover was put on the book.

Gutenberg had made one of the most important inventions in history. But he did not pay back his debt. The man to whom he owed money took over his printing press. Gutenberg retired. Little more is known about him. Yet his invention changed the world. Ideas could be shared faster and easier than ever before.

The Miracle of Movable Type

This is how Gutenberg's printing press worked:

Step 1: A man set the pieces of metal type into a stick to form a sentence. He put them in backwards order.

Step 2: The type pieces moved from the stick to a galley tray.

Step 3: The galley was put into a metal frame called a type form.

Step 4: The form was inked. A piece of paper was laid over it. The form was carried to the press.

Step 5: A hand crank pressed the type form under a wooden slab. This moved the ink from the type to the paper.

Step 6: The page was hung to let the damp ink dry.

The Miracle of Movable Type

1. Before Gutenberg invented the printing press there were

   a. fewer books than today.

   b. about the same number of books as today.

   c. more books than today.

2. The first book that Gutenberg printed was

   a. a book about the German mint.   b. a Bible.   c. about monks.

3. Gutenberg's printing press changed the world in a way most similar to the invention of the

   a. plow.   b. Internet.   c. wheel.

4. Gutenberg printed his first book in 1450. True or False? Explain.

_____

_____

_____

5. How many steps did it take to print and dry a page with Gutenberg's press? What was the third step?

_____

_____

_____

_____

6. Will the Worldwide Web bring about the end of book publishing? Why or why not?

_____

_____

_____

_____

Galileo's Discoveries About the Universe

For thousands of years people thought that the universe was a hollow ball—like the inside of a basketball. Earth was in the middle. The sun, the moon, and the planets went around it in a circle. The stars did not move. They were fixed in place on the inner wall of the "ball." About 1520, Nicolaus Copernicus found out that this theory was wrong. He watched the sky. He saw the way that the moon and planets moved. They did not seem to go around Earth. He started to think that Earth and other planets went around the sun. But he had no way to prove it.

The Roman Catholic Church controlled all learning in Europe. It did not like Copernicus's ideas. The Church stated that Earth was the center of the universe. Anyone who said otherwise was a heretic. And the Church could kill a heretic.

Galileo Galilei was a scientist. He wanted to know how things worked. He did experiments with gravity. He knew about Copernicus's idea. He agreed with him. But he could not prove it. Then in 1609 he met a man. The man showed him a new Dutch invention. It was a crude telescope. Galileo got excited. He could improve upon it! He made one with curved glass lenses. This made things appear 32 times larger.

Galileo used his telescope to watch the night sky. He kept records of the motion of the moon and planets. By 1613, he knew how things really worked. Earth and other planets moved around the sun. He wrote about his findings. The Church attacked him. He waited for things to settle down. Twenty years later he repeated his findings in another book. This time the Church arrested him. It found him guilty of being a heretic. He would burn at the stake! Galileo did not want to die. So he said that he had written lies. The Church put him under house arrest for the rest of his life. He could not go places or talk about his ideas.

But Galileo had changed the world. He showed other scientists that it was important to make careful observations and keep records. He created a useful telescope. And he showed people that they could question the Church.

Galileo's Discoveries About the Universe

Galileo's telescope was the best at the time. But it was not strong enough to show him all of the planets in our solar system. He only knew about six of the planets.

The Solar System According to Galileo

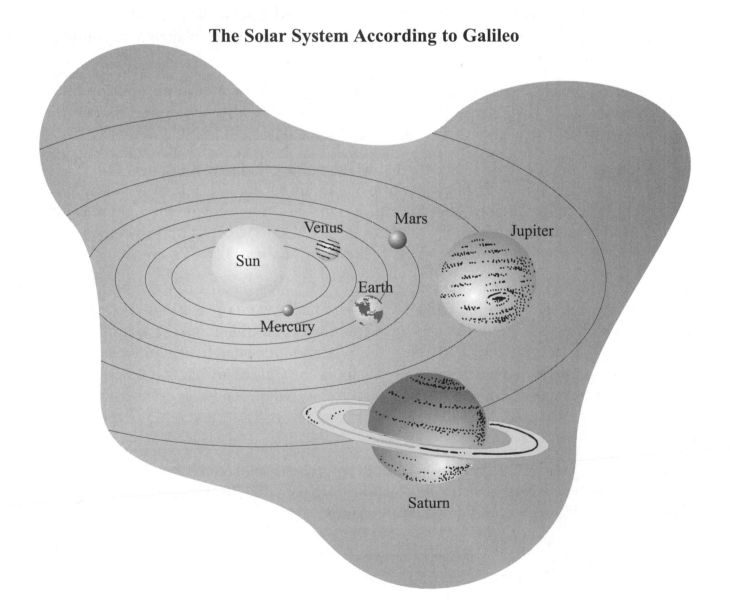

Galileo's Discoveries About the Universe

1. Galileo's ideas were attacked by
   a. other scientists.
   b. Nicolaus Copernicus.
   c. leaders of the Roman Catholic Church.

2. In what year did Galileo know for sure how our solar system is set up?
   a. 1520   b. 1609   c. 1613

3. Which planet did Galileo know about?
   a. Jupiter   b. Neptune   c. Uranus

4. In 1633 Galileo refused to say that what he had written about the sun and planets was wrong. True or False? Explain.

   _____

   _____

   _____

5. Look at Galileo's diagram of our solar system. Which planet is closest to the sun? Which one is fourth from the sun?

   _____

   _____

   _____

   _____

6. Should Galileo receive credit for inventing the telescope? Why or why not?

   _____

   _____

   _____

Dinosaurs

Did you know that a 13-year-old girl found the first dinosaur fossil? Mary Anning lived in Lyme Regis, England. It is near the seacoast. This area has big storms. When she was a baby, one ruined her home. And she was hit by lightning!

When she was older, Mary's dad took her and her brother Joe to hunt for fossils. They searched the nearby cliffs. They dug out fossils. They cleaned them. Then they put them on their front porch. Collectors bought them. In 1810, when Mary was just 11 years old, her dad died. This made the family poor. But the children found and sold fossils. One day she and Joe dug out a huge head. The children could not find the rest of the skeleton. But they were thrilled. They had never seen anything like it.

A bad storm hit in 1812. Loose rocks fell from the cliffs. The rest of the skeleton was exposed! Mary saw it. She paid men to help her dig it out. It was 20 feet long. She had just found the first dinosaur. Years later scientists named it Ichthyosaurus. This sea dinosaur swam in the sea millions of years ago.

Mary never married. She spent her life finding fossils. In 1823 she found a nearly complete skeleton of a Plesiosaurus. Five years later she found the first flying dinosaur fossil. It was a Pterosaur. Scientists bought these fossils. They studied them. Then they put them in museums.

During her life, people called Mary "The Fossil Woman." But she never wrote about her findings or sought any fame. Even today few books give her credit for discovering dinosaurs.

In 1844, Richard Owen coined the term *dinosaur*. It means terrible lizard. Mary Anning died just three years later. Now she is called the Princess of Paleontology. That's the word for the study of dinosaurs.

Dinosaurs

MANTELL, GIDEON (1790–1852), was one of the first fossil hunters. In 1822, his wife saw some teeth sticking out of a rock. She showed it to him. He knew that it was a fossil. But he had no idea what the animal was.

Mantell took the rock home. He studied it. The rock around the teeth was 130 million years old. He looked at animal skeletons to find a match. In 1824, he saw that the teeth looked like an iguana's. Mantell wrote an article. He called the animal Iguanadon. He stated that huge lizards had once walked on Earth. Because he shared his findings, he is usually given credit for finding the first dinosaur. Others credit Mary Anning. (See ANNING, MARY)

Nine years later, a whole Iguanadon skeleton was found. Mantell paid $40 for it. He spent months putting it together. He came close. But he put the two thumb claws on the forehead. He thought they were a pair of spiked horns.

Mantell wrote more articles about dinosaurs. He told about their teeth. Those with flat teeth, like the stegosaurus, ate plants. Those with pointed teeth, like the T-Rex, ate animals. He stated that dinosaurs were reptiles and laid eggs. (See DINOSAURS; PALEONTOLOGY)

Dinosaurs

1. A dinosaur fossil with flat teeth lets you know that the dinosaur

   a. laid eggs.   b. ate plants.   c. ate other animals.

2. What is something that paleontologists cannot tell from a fossil?

   a. the dinosaur's length   c. whether the dinosaur hunted
   b. the dinosaur's height   during the day or night

3. Picture yourself looking at an actual dinosaur skeleton set up on display. Where are you?

   a. at a school   b. at a museum   c. at a movie theater

4. Mary Anning found an Iguanadon skeleton. True or False? Explain.

_____

_____

_____

5. Why does Gideon Mantell get the credit for finding the first dinosaur in 1822 when Mary Anning found one in 1812?

_____

_____

_____

_____

6. If you could, which dinosaur would you most like to see in real life? Why?

_____

_____

_____

_____

Joseph Lister's Fight Against Germs

If germs get into our bodies, infection occurs. You may have had an infected cut. It happened after your skin was broken. This let germs in. If you've had an infected cut, a cream cured it. That's because we know what was wrong. But 150 years ago, doctors didn't know what caused infection. Their patients often died from it. But they had no idea why. This meant that they had no idea how to stop it.

Joseph Lister began working on the problem in 1860. He had read Louis Pasteur's work. This chemist had written about germs. Pasteur was the first person to find that these small cells can do great harm. Lister wondered how to fight germs.

He talked with other professors. What might kill germs? One said carbolic acid. In 1865 Lister started dressing wounds with carbolic acid. He found that it stopped infection. It helped healing, too. Using this method he could save injured arms and legs that would have been cut off. Next he found that sores and other skin infections could be cured the same way.

Soon doctors in many nations started to use his methods. They saw success and were thrilled. Word spread quickly. It had reached America by 1867. But many patients still died after surgery. Lister wondered if germs in the air let people get internal infections that could not be seen. He wanted to find a way to clean the air in operating rooms.

He made a carbolic acid pump. It sprayed a solution into the air during surgery. He also told doctors that they must wash their hands. They had to use clean clothes and tools for each operation. Before that, they had worn the same clothes and used the same scalpel all day long! Most of the time they did not even wash their hands or instruments between patients! Many doctors were annoyed by the extra work. Some would not do it. Yet those who tried Lister's ideas saw their death rate after surgery drop. Instead of one patient out of every three dying, it was one patient in 20.

Of course many advances have been made since that time. We have many ways to fight germs in our hospitals, homes, and schools. It all started with Joseph Lister and his desire to stop germs.

How Germs Spread

Germs can move from dirty hands to food. This happens when a person does not wash his or her hands before making or eating food.

Germs move from raw meat to a person's hands. If the person doesn't wash and touches the salad, the greens now have the germs. When the meat is cooked, the germs die. But the salad is not cooked, so the germs remain.

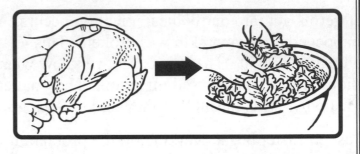

Germs can move from a sick person to a healthy one. This can happen if a person wipes his or her nose and then touches something. Then another person picks it up and gets the germs. Washing your hands when you are sick is really important.

Germs can also spread through the air. The best way to stop that is to cover every cough and sneeze with your hand or a tissue. Then wash your hands.

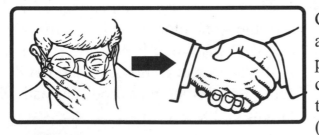

Germs that cause colds, and eye, ear, and throat pain can move from a sick person to a well one through hand contact. Always wash your hands after touching the part of you that feels ill (such as rubbing eyes).

As you can see, most germs spread on dirty hands. So wash your hands with soap and water often!

Joseph Lister's Fight Against Germs

1. Joseph Lister taught doctors to

 a. do operations.

 b. wash their hands and instruments between patients.

 c. use medicines to fight cancer.

2. How did doctors figure out that Joseph Lister's ideas were right?

 a. Fewer patients were dying after surgery, and fewer wounds were infected.

 b. People with cancer began to live longer.

 c. Fewer people needed to have operations.

3. How did Louis Pasteur help Joseph Lister?

 a. Lister read Pasteur's work on germs, which helped him start to find a way to fight them.

 b. In college Lister was Pasteur's student.

 c. Pasteur suggested the use of carbolic acid to Lister.

4. Lister used carbolic acid to prevent infection. True or False? Explain.

_____

_____

_____

5. What is the best thing you can do to keep from spreading germs? Why is it important for you to cover every sneeze and cough?

_____

_____

_____

_____

6. After doing this lesson, will you wash your hands more often than before? Why or why not?

_____

_____

_____

_____

The Janitor's Invention

Are all inventors scientists? No. Anyone can make an invention. All it takes is an idea and some hard work. A person must be willing to try again and again until the invention works. That's just what happened to Murray Spangler in 1907.

Spangler was a janitor at a department store. Every night after the store closed, he went to work. He took pride in his job. But it was a lot of work to clean all that space. So his back and feet ached. His muscles hurt. He wished that there was a better way to clean the store's floor.

Spangler lived during a time when new machines were being invented almost daily. Each night as he worked, he thought about the problem. What kind of a machine could he make? After a while, some ideas formed in his head. He got an old box, tape, a pillowcase, an electric fan, a broom handle, a stove pipe, and a paint roller. He added stiff goat bristles to the roller. Then he spent time assembling and adjusting his machine. It took several weeks. He tried it at home. It worked! At last, he was ready to take his invention to the store.

A police officer was walking down the street. He glanced in the department store window. He saw Spangler using his invention. The officer went to the owner's house and woke him up. He told the owner that Spangler was doing something with an odd-looking contraption that made a lot of noise. He thought that Spangler had lost his mind!

The owner rushed to the store. He told Spangler that he was fired for messing around instead of doing his job. Spangler told him that he was doing his job—better than ever before. He asked the storeowner to let him demonstrate. Curious, the man agreed. He was shocked when Spangler moved his machine over dirt and gum wrappers. They disappeared! Spangler had just built the first vacuum cleaner. The next year he sold his invention to a firm named Hoover. Before long vacuum cleaners were as common as stoves in homes.

The Janitor's Invention

This Hoover vacuum ad appeared in 1921 in *National Geographic* magazine:

The annoying dust that so steadily drifts into the home and settles upon upholstery and portieres or collects out of convenient reach, may be easily and dustlessly suctioned away by the *new* long-armed air attachments of The Hoover. But to clean rugs with the thoroughness that invariably adds years to their life and beauty, more than air is essential. So The Hoover gently beats rugs to remove all nap-wearing, buried grit. Swiftly it sweeps up stubbornest litter, lifts crushed nap and revives colors. Powerfully it suction cleans. Only The Hoover does all these things; therefore, only The Hoover repeatedly pays for itself by protecting valuable rugs from avoidable wear. And it is the largest-selling electric cleaner in the world.

The HOOVER

It Beats — as it Sweeps — as it Cleans

Write for booklet, "How to Judge an Electric Cleaner," and names of Authorized Dealers licensed to sell and service Hoovers bearing our guarantee

The Hoover Suction Sweeper Company, Factories at North Canton, Ohio, and Hamilton, Ontario

The Hoover lifts the rug from the floor, like this—gently beats out its embedded grit, and so prolongs its life

"Mention The Geographic—It identifies you"

The Janitor's Invention

1. Which thing was not a part of Murray Spangler's original vacuum cleaner?

    a. a cloth bag   b. an electric fan   c. a stove pipe

2. Murray Spangler invented the vacuum cleaner because he wanted to

    a. make his job easier.   b. get rich.   c. win a bet with the store owner.

3. The police officer who saw the janitor vacuuming thought that Murray Spangler was doing something

    a. boring.   b. illegal.   c. wrong.

4. In 1921 Hoover was not the only company making vacuum cleaners.   True or False? Explain.

_____

_____

_____

5. Read the Hoover advertisement. What were vacuum cleaners called in 1921? What reasons does the ad give for vacuuming rugs?

_____

_____

_____

6. Do you like using new gadgets? Why or why not?

_____

_____

_____

Recycling

Have you ever thought about the fact that most of what you own will one day be thrown out? Think about your clothes, the TV, and the stove. They will tear or break down. Or you may just want to get new, better things. But where do things go when you throw them out?

The bad news is that most of it goes to a landfill. A landfill is a big hole in the ground. It may have a concrete or plastic liner. This liner keeps chemicals from seeping into the groundwater around the landfill. Trash trucks filled with all the things that people throw out go to the landfill. They dump their loads into the hole. Bulldozers cover everything with soil. But there is a better way. And since we are running out of landfill space, more people are doing it.

The better way is recycling. Recycling lets things be used again. Give away an old TV or stove. They can be fixed so that someone else can use them. Clothes can be sent to people who need them. Most glass, paper, plastic, and metal is recyclable. When people recycle these things, it helps the environment. It saves space in landfills. (Paper takes up more space in landfills than any other thing!) And instead of wasting these materials, they get used again.

Some people have recycle bins. They put their paper, metal, glass, and plastic into the bin. A special truck takes these things to a processing center. Other people must drive to a recycling center and drop off their things.

What happens at the recycling center? Paper is shredded and then mixed with water and wood pulp to make new paper. Glass, metal, and plastics are melted down. Then they are poured into molds to form new things. Glass jars are melted down and become new glass jars. Recycling lets things be used over and over.

Have you ever heard of a car crusher? First the tires and windows are removed from an old car. Then it enters the crusher. Powerful jaws smash the car. It comes out a small, flattened rectangle. Then it is loaded onto a train car. It goes to a place where the steel is melted down and used to make new cars.

This symbol means a thing can be recycled.

This symbol means a thing is made from recycled things.

Recycling

Plastic Item	Marked	Can Be Made Into
Soda bottles, food product packaging, oven-ready meal trays, and vitamin bottles	♳ 1 PETE	Soda bottles, paint brushes, carpeting, microfleece for clothing and blankets; fiber filling for sleeping bags, comforters, coats, and vests
Milk, juice, and water jugs, shampoo, detergent, and other cleaning fluid bottles	♴ 2 HDPE	Milk, juice, and water jugs, drainage pipes, trash cans, and the fibers used in bullet-proof vests
Clear food wrap, cooking oil bottles, molded plastic lawn chairs	♵ 3 PVC	Recyclable plastics marked 3–7 are mixed together and used to make big plastic items such as picnic tables, sand boxes, plumbing pipes, fencing, park benches, playground equipment, plastic lumber, lawn chairs, storage bins, etc.
Rings for 6-packs, coffee can lids, grocery store bags, and trash can liners	♶ 4 LDPE	
Margarine and whipped topping tubs, yogurt cups, snap-on lids, and microwaveable meal trays	♷ 5 PP	
Styrofoam meat trays, egg cartons, and cups, insulation, plastic forks, spoons, and knives, and packing "peanuts"	♸ 6 PS	
Squeeze bottles for jellies, sauces, and syrups, and various other plastics	♹ 7 Other	

Recycling

1. What happens to glass jars that you throw out instead of recycle?

   a. People dig through the trash, find them, and send them to a recycling center.

   b. They take up space in a landfill.

   c. They slowly rot and turn back into soil.

2. A car crusher is used as the first step in recycling a car's

   a. windows and windshield.   b. tires.   c. metal.

3. What is the most important reason to recycle paper?

   a. It saves trees from being cut down.

   b. It will keep us from running out of paper.

   c. It keeps the cost of paper low.

4. Plastics marked "3" and "4" can be recycled to make fabrics. True or False? Explain.

_____

_____

_____

5. Name three kinds of plastic items that are labeled "6."

_____

_____

_____

_____

6. If you could only recycle one: glass, metal, paper, or plastic, which would be the most important one? Why?

_____

_____

_____

_____

Earth's Hot Spots

Did you know that Yellowstone National Park lies above one of the Earth's "hot spots"? A hot spot is where melted rock from Earth's core comes within four miles of its crust. High heat turns water below the ground into steam. This hot water and steam blows up through holes. These places are called geysers. There are only about 600 on Earth. And 400 of those are in Yellowstone.

A geyser is like a rock "pipe" that goes deep into the Earth. The pipe stretches down to a reservoir that holds hot ground water. As the heat builds up, the water turns to steam. It needs to escape, just as steam does from a tea kettle. As soon as there is enough steam, it shoots up the tube and spurts into the air like a fountain.

Some geysers explode every couple of days. Others do so after years. They cannot be predicted. However, one Yellowstone geyser, Old Faithful, erupts every 77 minutes. It has done so for hundreds of years. Each time it shoots water into the sky for 3 to 5 minutes.

Geysers aren't the only things that lie above hot spots. Hot springs do, too. There are places in Japan and Iceland where people can soak in a natural "hot tub" year round. The people do not get burned because the hot water mixes with cooler water near the ground's surface. In a few places the water mixes with dirt to form hot mud baths. Some people think that soaking in hot mud cures illnesses.

The world's most talked about hot spots are volcanoes. Many volcanoes erupt each day. But no one sees them. They are on the sea floor. Surtsey, the world's newest island, started as an undersea volcano. The volcano spilled lava on the sea floor. The lava cooled. It formed rock. Over a long time the lava built up. It grew into a mountain. When it broke the sea's surface, it became an island. All of the Hawaiian Islands formed this way.

Old Faithful

Earth's Hot Spots

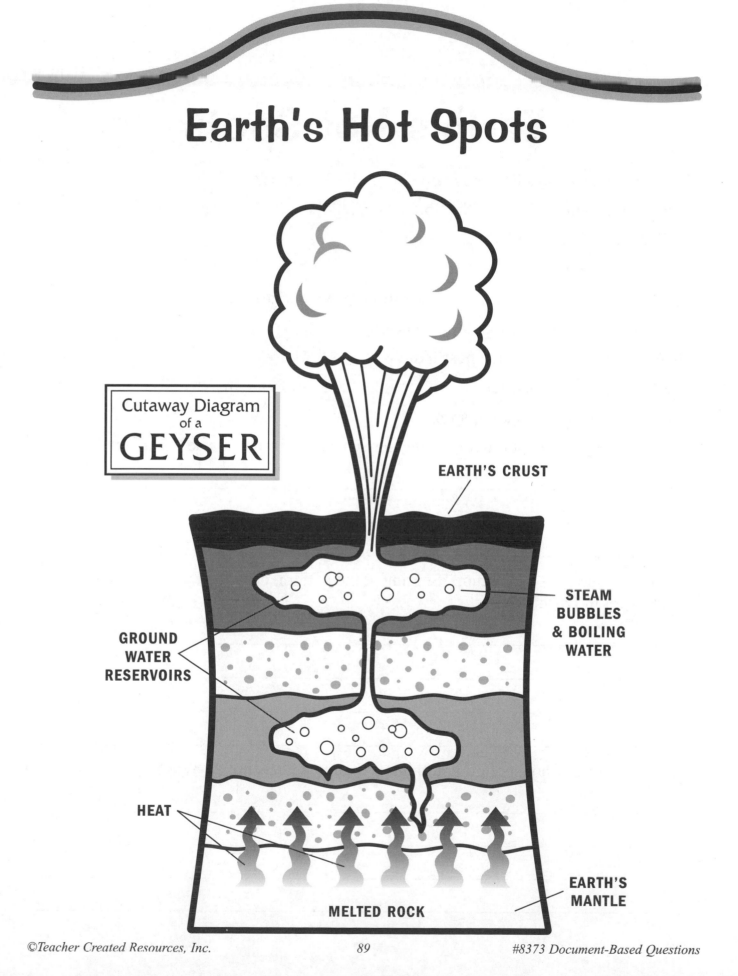

Cutaway Diagram
of a
GEYSER

EARTH'S CRUST

STEAM BUBBLES & BOILING WATER

GROUND WATER RESERVOIRS

HEAT

EARTH'S MANTLE

MELTED ROCK

Earth's Hot Spots

1. Which one always lies above one of Earth's hot spots?

   a. a mud bath   b. an island   c. a river

2. How are geysers and volcanoes alike?

   a. Both send out lava.

   b. Both erupt from heat that comes from below the ground.

   c. Both cause hot springs to form nearby.

3. A geyser erupting looks most like

   a. a whistling tea kettle.   c. a tall fountain.

   b. steam rising from a hot spring.

4. Most geysers do not erupt on a regular schedule. True or False? Explain.

   _____

   _____

   _____

5. Look at the geyser diagram. Starting at the bottom, describe the layers beneath this hot spot in Earth's crust.

   _____

   _____

   _____

   _____

6. Which type of hot spot do you think is the most interesting? Why?

   _____

   _____

   _____

   _____

Big Blast in Siberia

Did you know that no one knows what caused the largest natural blast on Earth? It happened on June 30, 1908. The place was Tunguska, Siberia. This part of Russia is quite cold. Few people live there. No one is sure just what occurred. But all agree that it was good that it happened where it did. In other places it would have caused great loss of life. And no buildings would have been left intact.

The blast's power was shocking. It knocked down people, cows, and horses over 400 miles away! It flattened and burned everything within 24 miles of its center. Not one tree or building remained standing. Trees lay on the ground around a center point. They looked like spokes on a bike wheel.

Some people said that they saw a thing fall from the sky. This was a few seconds before the blast. Then there was such a bright light that they had to shield their eyes. For two months after the blast, people saw odd-colored sunsets. Streaks of green and bright yellow filled the sky all over Europe. And the nights never got dark. People could read outside at midnight!

Scientists have some ideas about what happened. But they cannot prove them. High radiation levels were measured at the site. This lasted for many years. It was an atomic explosion. Yet it occurred 36 years before humans made the first atom bomb. And it was more destructive than that first atom bomb. Small crystals found in asteroids have been found at the site, too. The most likely answer is that an asteroid blew up when it entered Earth's atmosphere. That would cause a natural atomic explosion. And it would explain why there's no crater (big hole in the ground).

Researchers say that the object weighed 10,000 tons. But we may never know for sure what it was.

Big Blast in Siberia

This is a Native American's eyewitness account. Chuchan of the Shanyagir tribe was dozens of miles from the Siberian blast and survived to tell about it. In 1926, Chuchan told his story to I. M. Suslov, who wrote it down:

"We had a hut by the river with my brother Chekaren. We were sleeping. Suddenly we both woke up at the same time . . . We heard whistling and felt strong wind. Chekaren said, "Can you hear all those birds flying overhead?" We were both in the hut, couldn't see what was going on outside.

Suddenly, I got shoved . . . . so hard I fell into the fire. I got scared. Chekaren got scared, too. We started crying out for father, mother, brother. But no one answered. There was noise beyond the hut. We could hear trees falling down. Me and Chekaren got out of our sleeping bags and wanted to run out, but then the thunder struck. This was the first thunder. The Earth began to move and rock. Wind hit our hut and knocked it over. My body was pushed down by sticks, but my head was in the clear.

Then I saw a wonder: Trees were falling, their branches were on fire. It became mighty bright, how can I say this, as if there was a second sun. My eyes were hurting. I even closed them. It was like what the Russians call lightning. And immediately there was a loud thunderclap. This was the second thunder. The morning was sunny. There were no clouds. Our sun was shining brightly as usual, and suddenly there came a second one!

Me and Chekaren had some difficulty getting from under the remains of our hut. Then we saw that above, but in a different place, there was another flash, and loud thunder came. This was the third thunder strike. Wind came again, knocked us off our feet, struck against the fallen trees.

We looked at the fallen trees, watched the treetops get snapped off, watched the fires. Suddenly Chekaren yelled, "Look up!" and pointed with his hand. I looked there and saw another flash, and it made another thunder. But the noise was less than before. This was the fourth strike, like normal thunder.

Now I remember well there was also one more thunder strike. But it was small, and somewhere far away, where the sun goes to sleep."

Big Blast in Siberia

1. The big blast in Siberia in 1907 was probably caused by an

    a. atomic bomb.   b. asteroid.   c. earthquake.

2. The big blast occurred in a

    a. city.   b. suburb.   c. place where few people lived.

3. The Siberian explosion caused changes that people could see in the

    a. sky.   b. oceans.   c. Himalayan mountains.

4. Chekaren pushed Chuchan into the fire. True or False? Explain.

_____

_____

_____

5. How many thunder strikes did Chuchan hear? Were they caused by a thunderstorm? How do you know?

_____

_____

_____

6. Which is more important in determining what caused the blast: eyewitness accounts or scientific observations (like the level of radiation at the site)? Why?

_____

_____

_____

The Story of the Brooklyn Bridge

Did you know that there is an amazing story behind the famous Brooklyn Bridge? The man who came up with the idea for the bridge died before he could start building it. Twenty workers died making it. And the builders' leader got so sick that he never recovered! His wife became the first female construction foreman in America.

The Brooklyn Bridge joins the island of Brooklyn to the main part of New York City. It has two large stone towers. They stand on solid rock under the East River. Big cables are hooked onto these towers. These cables hold up the road. The road actually hangs in midair!

In 1869, John Roebling went to the river. He wanted to find the best spot for the bridge. While he was on a dock, a boat crushed his foot against the edge. His wound got infected. He died a few weeks later. His son, Washington, said he would build the bridge. But after working on the bridge's foundation, he got very sick. He had worked in a compression chamber under the water. The chamber was like a huge box. It was sunk into the river. Air was pumped into the box to keep it dry. Men worked inside the box to lay the bridge's foundation. But working inside the chamber was dangerous. Several men became invalids. And Roebling got so ill that he never went back again. Instead he watched the work from his bedroom window.

He sent his wife, Emily Roebling, to lead the workers. Back then women did not work on building projects. So no woman had ever been in charge! At first the men did not want to listen to her. But over time they began to respect her. She brought directions from Roebling every day. On his worst days he could not speak. Then he tapped the message into her hand.

In May 1883 the Brooklyn Bridge opened. At that time it was the longest suspension bridge in the world. There was a big party. Roebling had had the workers make the bridge very strong. It's a good thing, too. Today the bridge carries many more cars than anyone could imagine back then. People cross it on foot. They walk on a raised platform above the traffic.

Courtesy of the Library of Congress, "New York City: Brooklyn Bridge from Brooklyn view," LC-USZ62-79048

The Story of the Brooklyn Bridge

The Brooklyn Bridge and the Towns' Wedding

Let all of the bells ring clear!
Let all of the flags be seen!
The King of the Western Hemisphere[1]
Has married the Island Queen.[2]
For many a day he waited
By the shining river's side,
Certain the island was fated
To be his own true bride.

People were always dashing
From him to his adored.
But the river lay flashing
Between them, like a sword.
In heart they were well mated.
And patiently and long
They for each other waited.
These lovers true and strong.

Now let no flag be hidden!
And let no bell be dumb![3]
The guests have all been bidden.[4]
The wedding now has come.

Through many a golden year
Shall shine this silvery tie.
The wondering world will gather here
To gaze with gleaming eye.
And praise 1883, the year
When in May, a month so green,
The King of the Western Hemisphere
Was wed to the Island Queen.

[1]New York City   [2]town of Brooklyn   [3]silent   [4]invited

An adaptation of *The Wedding of the Towns* by Will Carleton first published in *The Independent* on Thursday, May 24, 1883, Vol. XXXV, No. 1799.

The Story of the Brooklyn Bridge

1. In the late 1800s where was the world's longest suspension bridge built?

    a. in Washington   b. in Roebling   c. in New York City

2. What happened last?

    a. John Roebling worked on the project.

    b. Emily Roebling worked on the project.

    c. Washington Roebling worked on the project.

3. Why was the Brooklyn Bridge so important in 1883?

    a. It showed that suspension bridges could span wide rivers.

    b. It was beautiful.

    c. It proved that Americans could build bridges.

4. Read the poem. Before the "wedding," people used horses and carriages to dash between the "King" and his adored "Queen." True or False? Explain.

    _____

    _____

    _____

5. Read the poem. Who is the Island Queen? Who is the King of the Western Hemisphere? What is the silvery tie that joins the two?

    _____

    _____

    _____

    _____

6. Do you think that bridge construction workers today would accept Emily Roebling as their leader? Why or why not?

    _____

    _____

    _____

    _____

Libraries Make the World a Smarter Place

Do you like going to your school or public library? You know that you can take out books and other things. It's free. You only have to pay if you lose an item or bring it back late. Public libraries have made knowledge available to all people.

It wasn't always this way. Years ago, just the rich had libraries. They had rooms in their homes that held thousands of books. But they only lent them to friends. A few towns had libraries. But a person had to pay to borrow the books. Colleges had libraries, too. But just their students could use them.

Andrew Carnegie was a very rich man. He said that each person could improve by learning. He wanted anyone to be able to use a library. So in 1919 he gave the funds to build 1,700 public libraries. They went up all over the United States.

Each library must keep track of what it owns. When a new book comes in, a worker stamps the library's name inside it. The book's title, author, and price are put in the accession record. This is a list of each item the library has ever had. So a book entered today may have a big number. The worker often writes the book's accession number on its title page.

Next the book's information is put into a card catalog. This is usually stored on computer. A bar code is glued inside the book. A sticker with the book's location gets glued on the book's spine. If it is a nonfiction (true) book, it gets a Dewey Decimal number. It tells where the book should go on a shelf. For example, books with the Dewey Decimal number 636 are about pets.

Sometimes a plastic jacket gets taped to the book. This protects the cover. At last the book is put on a shelf. Now it's ready for you to check out!

Courtesy of the Library of Congress, "Library of Congress," LC-D43-T01-15061

Did You Know?

Libraries Make the World a Smarter Place

The Dewey Decimal System is how most public libraries shelve their nonfiction (true) books. Using decimals allows an endless amount of books to be numbered. That's a good thing. New books are published every day.

Numbers	Called	Examples	
000–099	Generalities	030 060 070	Encyclopedias Museums Journalism and Publishing
100–199	Philosophy and Psychology	133.1 150 160	Ghosts Self-help Logic
200–299	Religion	220 292	Bible Myths
300–399	Social Sciences	340 392.5 398	Law Weddings Folk and Fairy Tales
400–499	Languages	413 419 460	Dictionaries Sign Language Spanish
500–599	Natural Sciences and Math	551.5 552 598	Weather Rocks and Minerals Birds
600–699	Technology (Applied Sciences)	610 629.1 641.5	Medicine Airplanes Cooking
700–799	The Arts and Sports	740 769 796.332	Drawing Stamp Collecting Football
800–899	Literature	811 812 840	Poetry Plays French Literature
900–999	Geography and History	912 932 973.7	Maps and Atlases Ancient Rome The American Civil War

Libraries Make the World a Smarter Place

1. Some of the U.S. public libraries were built with money given by

a. a foreign government.   b. Melvil Dewey.   c. Andrew Carnegie.

2. A Dewey Decimal number tells library workers

a. where to find a book in the library.   c. if they can afford to buy a book.

b. the date a book was published.

3. If people do not have a chance to read books, they may

a. get sick.   b. find a better job.   c. not get to learn new things.

4. A card catalog contains information about all of the books that a library owns. True or False? Explain._____

_____

_____

5. Look at the chart. Under what Dewey Decimal number would you look to find books about different types of birds? Where would you look to find books about how to play football? Where would you look to find an atlas?

_____

_____

_____

_____

6. Do you prefer reading fiction books or nonfiction (true) books? Why?

_____

_____

_____

_____

Lightships

Did you know that the U.S. Coast Guard used lightships from 1821 to 1983? These ships were like moveable lighthouses. They were used where a lighthouse could not be built. They would anchor in a place with an underwater hazard. It might be a sandbar or rocks. A lightship might also mark the entry to harbors, rivers, and bays. Each ship had a bright light. It also had a loud foghorn. During fog, the constant noise from it blasted the sailors who lived on board.

The men who served on lightships spent 30 days at sea. Then they had 10 days of shore leave. Their life was unusual. Most of the time it was dull. They read or played cards. But at other times being on a lightship was scary. They had to ride out hurricanes and other bad storms. They could not move to safety. They had to stay in place to warn others. In November 1913, *Lightship 82* sprang a leak during a big storm on Lake Erie. It sank. All the men aboard died. Over the years a total of 12 lightships sank, and 150 were seriously damaged in storms or accidents.

In 1920, lightships started sending out radio signals. They were meant to guide other ships. But sometimes they led ships right to the lightships. The other ships ran into them! The *Olympia* was as big as the *Titanic*. In 1934 the *Olympia* hit *Lightship 117*. This happened in dense fog off Cape Cod. The lightship was cut in half. Seven of its 11 sailors died.

Lightships are no longer used. Lighted buoys have taken their place. Now ships have a better idea of where they are at all times. They use global positioning systems (GPS). With GPS, a ship knows its exact location. And each ship's captain gets up-to-date information on underwater hazards by computer or radio.

Courtesy of the Library of Congress,
"Light Ship," LC-DIG-ggbain-04043

Lightships

On June 24, 1960, the *SS Green Bay* struck the U.S. Coast Guard Lightship *Relief.* This is a letter from a sailor aboard the *Relief:*

Dear Mom and Dad and all,   June 25, 1960

I wanted to give you more details about the collision we suffered yesterday. About 4:10 in the morning we were in dense fog. Suddenly the freighter SS Green Bay struck us with such force that we all fell to the deck. Those sleeping were thrown from their bunks.

We had a starboard[1] hole 12 feet long and 2 feet wide. We had no time to send an SOS or to save anything, even the logbook. Captain Tamalonis told us to abandon ship. Our motor lifeboat had been ripped away in the crash. Bobbie launched the self-inflating rubber life raft. The men who'd been asleep rushed to get their pants and wallets.

Bobbie put the ladder over the side, and I climbed down into the raft. The rest of the crew followed me. The Relief was already so low in the water that the Captain just stepped from the deck onto our raft! We paddled away as fast as we could. We feared that when the Relief went under, she'd take us down with her undertow. If she rolled over, her masts or rigging could hit us.

At 4:21 A.M. the Relief sank beneath the waves. She went stern first. It was hard to believe that so few minutes had passed since the Green Bay rammed her. All nine of us sat in silence. We all worried what would happen next since we were drifting in heavy fog in the Atlantic's busiest shipping lane. We heard the Green Bay drop anchor. But we couldn't see her through the fog. Her crew shouted to us. They sounded their horn and bell. We fired flares and yelled. We tried to paddle towards the freighter's sounds. But it was hard to get our bearings, as sound is dampened in fog. We just could not find the ship.

After about an hour in the lifeboat, a huge ocean liner appeared and almost ran us down. It was the Queen Elizabeth! She came so close we felt sure we were goners. Captain Tamalonis fired 30 flares. We blew whistles and shouted until we were hoarse. We read her name as she slowly moved by. Our life raft rocked wildly in her wake.

At last, around 5:30 A.M., a motor lifeboat from the Green Bay found us. What a welcome sight! It towed us over to the Green Bay. The freighter had not sustained much damage. About an hour later, a U.S. Coast Guard Harbor Entrance Patrol Boat arrived and took us back to the St. George U.S. Coast Guard Base. I was glad to step ashore.

I miss you all. Don't worry about me. The worst is past!

William

[1] the right side of the ship when one is facing it head on

Lightships

1. When did the U.S. Coast Guard lightships begin using radio signals?

   a. 1913   b. 1920   c. 1934

2. What has replaced lightships?

   a. lighted buoys and GPS.   c. two-way radios.

   b. automated lighthouses.

3. What was one of the worst hazards faced by lightships and their crews?

   a. ice cold water   b. thunder   c. thick fog

4. When a storm was coming, lightships could not seek a safe harbor. True or False? Explain.

   _____

   _____

   _____

5. Read William's letter. How much time passed between when the *Green Bay* struck the *Relief* and when the lightship sank? What actions did the *Relief's* crew take to try to reach the *Green Bay*?

   _____

   _____

   _____

   _____

6. Do you think that the crew of the *Queen Elizabeth* saw the men in the *Relief's* life raft? Tell why.

   _____

   _____

   _____

   _____

Mount Rushmore

Did you know that there is a cliff in South Dakota with four men's heads carved into it? It is the world's biggest sculpture. Its name is Mount Rushmore. It took workers 14 years to form the heads. Each one is 60 feet tall! They had to drill, chip, and blast to shape the rock into faces. The rocks they knocked away lie in a big pile far below the heads. The work was hard. But the men wore ropes to stay safe.

The heads show George Washington, Thomas Jefferson, Theodore Roosevelt, and Abraham Lincoln. Each man was a U.S. president. Mount Rushmore honors these leaders. Why? Each one did something important for America.

George Washington led the Revolutionary War. After it, the nation was free to make its own laws. Then he led America as its first president.

Thomas Jefferson wrote the Declaration of Independence. It told Great Britain that Americans would rule themselves. Later he was chosen to be the third president. He bought a big piece of land. It lay west of the Mississippi River. It doubled the size of the nation.

In the 1860s the states in the south tried to break away from the United States. They wanted to form their own nation. Abraham Lincoln wanted to keep the nation united. It caused a war, but America stayed united. Lincoln also set all slaves free in 1863. He said that one person could not own another.

Theodore Roosevelt started building the Panama Canal. This let ships go between the Atlantic and Pacific Oceans. People and things could move faster than ever before. He set aside parts of America as national parks, too. This way anyone could enjoy them. If he had not done this, a rich person could have bought the Grand Canyon! Then other people could not have gone there. Mount Rushmore is one of these national parks.

Mount Rushmore

Frequently Asked Questions About Mount Rushmore

1. Who created the sculpture?

Gutzon Borglum and 400 workers.

2. What did the sculpture cost?

$989,992.32.

3. How long did it take to build?

14 years (October 4, 1927–October 31,1941)

4. Are the faces eroding?

No. The rock is hard. The erosion rate is one inch every 10,000 years.

5. Who is the mountain named after?

Charles E. Rushmore, a New York City lawyer, who was in South Dakota on business in 1885.

6. Were there any deaths during the carving?

No.

Ownership

Information presented on this website, unless otherwise indicated, is considered in the public domain. It may be distributed or copied as is permitted by the law.

Mount Rushmore National Park Service web site, **http://www.nps.gov/disclaimer.htm**

Mount Rushmore

1. Mount Rushmore is a cliff in

   a. Panama.　　　　　b. Mississippi.　　　　　c. South Dakota.

2. Theodore Roosevelt is famous because he

   a. wrote the Declaration of Independence.　　c. freed the slaves.

   b. started the national park system.

3. Why aren't the heads placed in order of the men's presidencies?

   a. Each head was placed where the rock could be most easily shaped into that person's face.

   b. No one knew the order in which the men had served as U.S. presidents.

   c. The job was done before the sculptor realized that heads weren't in the right order.

4. Mount Rushmore is named after a famous U.S. president. True or False? Explain.

_____

_____

_____

5. Will the faces wear away from weathering during your lifetime? Explain.

_____

_____

_____

_____

6. Would you like to go see Mount Rushmore? Why or why not?

_____

_____

_____

_____

Answer Key

Page 12

1. a   2. c   3. c

4. False. An emperor penguin eats more fish than any other food. In fact, 95 of every 100 meals it eats is fish. Just two out of every 100 meals are krill.

5. The Emperor penguins would have to find more fish and krill to eat if all of the squid in their area died. Fewer penguins might survive because there would be less food for them. But since just three out of every 100 meals are squid, it probably wouldn't hurt the penguin population too badly.

6. Yes, it's good that the emperor penguins have just one baby each year because there is only room for one in the broodpouch. And the parents only have to come up with enough food to keep one baby alive. OR No, it's not good that the emperor penguins have just one baby each year because this means that they reproduce slowly. The fewer penguins that are born, the fewer that survive. This might be bad for the species' survival.

Page 15

1. a   2. c   3. a

4. True. The Venus flytrap has traps that close tightly and form a seal to keep out germs and mold. OR True. If one of the traps gets infected, it will fall off the plant. This keeps the disease from spreading.

5. In step one, the trap is ready to catch a bug. In step four the trap has just finished eating a bug. It must wait for rain or wind to wash the remains away before it can trap another one.

6. Yes, I'd like to have a Venus flytrap as a house plant because I think it is an interesting plant; pretty; unusual; I would like to see it trap and eat a bug; it would help get rid of the mosquitoes that get into our house; etc. OR No, I wouldn't want to have a Venus flytrap as a house plant because there aren't enough bugs in my house to keep it alive, so I'd have to bring it food; the fact that it eats bugs is gross; I don't like house plants; I think they belong in the wild, etc.

Page 18

1. a   2. c   3. b

4. False. It takes less than two weeks for platypus eggs to hatch. OR False. It takes just 10 days for platypus eggs to hatch.

5. A platypus first looks for a mate when it is 2 years old.

6. Yes, I agree with the law that says no one can hunt platypuses because they became endangered when hunting was allowed. It's a good thing that they are now protected. OR No, I disagree with the law that says no one can hunt platypuses because if their numbers are not kept under control, there may get to be too many of them. Then some would starve. This has happened with deer (woodchucks, armadillos, Canadian geese, etc.) when hunting was stopped.

Page 21

1. c   2. a   3. b

4. True. Kelp provides algin. This thickening agent is used in tires, ice cream, and other products.

5. Kelp forests do not grow along the coast of Europe. This is because the growing conditions are not right for it there. Kelp plants need shallow, clear seawater. They need rocky coasts, and the water must be the right temperature. (any three conditions)

6. Yes, methane made from kelp will someday replace gasoline because we are running out of gas and its cost is rising. This means that people will be willing to use methane instead, especially if it is cheaper. OR No, methane made from kelp will not replace gasoline because enough kelp cannot be grown fast enough to meet the world's demands for a gasoline substitute. People would destroy the wild kelp forests rapidly, which would mess up the environment. Kelp may eventually provide some methane, but not all of it.

Page 24

1. b   2. a   3. c

4. True. Cheetahs do not attack humans. Ancient royalty kept these big cats as pets.

5. Cheetahs used to live in Asia and Africa. Now they just live in Africa.

6. Yes, it is good that a law now prevents cheetahs from being pets because there are too few cheetahs already. If people could keep them as pets, they would be taken from the wild because they don't like to breed in captivity. After a while there would be no more wild cheetahs. Also, most people don't have the place or knowledge to keep such a big cat. OR No, it is bad that a law now prevents cheetahs from being pets because if they were allowed to be pets people would care more about the fact that they are endangered. Also, making it illegal means that people who want a pet cheetah bad enough will use illegal methods to get one.

Answer Key *(cont.)*

Page 27

1. a 2. b 3. a

4. False. The part of the cashew plant that is poisonous is the oil around the nut. The fruit and the nut itself are both good to eat.

5. It is more dangerous to breathe the smoke of burning poison ivy because it can give a person poison ivy of the lungs. This is so serious that it takes six weeks in a hospital to cure. Breathing the smoke of the roasting cashews will only cause eye and skin irritation.

6. Yes, plants like rhododendrons should be planted in public parks because they are beautiful. People may not have a yard or have room for them in their yard, so the only place where they will see such plants is in a public park. It's not very dangerous because it's rare to hear of someone poisoned by eating a public park plant. OR No, plants like rhododendrons should not be planted in public parks because they are poisonous. Most people do not know which plants are poisonous and which ones aren't. People take their children and dogs to public parks to walk around and play. If a pet or a child were to eat a part of the rhododendron, they might become so ill that they would have to go to the hospital. And the parent might not even realize what caused the problem, which would make it harder for the doctor to figure out how to cure.

Page 30

1. a 2. b 3. b

4. True. In 1866, Nellie lived in Mexico and wrote for the *Pittsburgh Dispatch*, and in 1914 she went to Austria to write about World War I.

5. In 1887 Nellie went undercover in an insane asylum. Nellie went undercover in an employment agency, a box-making factory, and a chorus line in 1888. (Accept any two dates and events.)

6. Yes, I would enjoy being a newspaper reporter because I like to write; it would give me a chance to travel; I enjoy reading and watching the news, etc. OR No, I would not enjoy being a newspaper reporter because I don't like writing; I would not like to travel; sometimes they are in danger; I don't like reading or watching the news, etc. (Allow reasonable responses.)

Page 33

1. a 2. c 3. b

4. True. Ice blocked it so much of the time that very few ships used it. OR False. Only once the passage had been found could people be sure that it was too hard to use as a sea route.

5. Amundsen sailed through the Bering Strait as part of the Northwest Passage. It separates Siberia (Russia) from Alaska (the United States). (Allow the specific names or nation names.)

6. Yes, Amundsen should have received a cash prize for finding the Northwest Passage because it was a major achievement that many men before him had tried and failed. And winning money would have helped him to pay for the costs of the trip (supplies, crew's pay, etc.). OR No, Amundsen shouldn't have received a cash prize for finding the Northwest Passage because he didn't go there expecting to be paid. He was an explorer who wanted to see if he could find the passage. Also, the Passage did not turn out to be useful, so it wasn't as if the discovery changed the world or made things better.

Page 36

1. c 2. a 3. b

4. False. The original race was run during January and the annual race is now held in March.

5. The dog sled teams had to cross the frozen water of the Yukon River and Norton Sound.

6. I would prefer to be a musher at this year's Iditarod because I love dogs and would enjoy racing them; I like the winter; I enjoy competitions/races, etc. OR I would prefer to be a spectator at this year's Iditarod because I am afraid of dogs; I don't like the cold; I don't enjoy competitions/races; it's dangerous; it would take too long to learn how to get a dog sled team to work together, etc.

Page 39

1. c 2. c 3. b

4. True. Twenty zoo animals died from the cold. And the snow drifted along the reindeer's fence. Three were able to step right over the fence and walk away from the zoo. (Give credit for either answer.)

5. It took the whole month of February (28 days) to remove all the snow from the city of Buffalo.

6. Yes, Larry Ramunno and his officers should have received the Carnegie Medal for Bravery because they risked their lives during a bad blizzard to save others. These men bravely faced the risk of frostbite and freezing to death. The people on the bridge probably would not have survived if the police hadn't come to their aid. OR No, Larry Ramunno and his officers should not have received the Carnegie Medal for Bravery because what they did was not dangerous enough. The men had on snowsuits to protect them from the cold,

Answer Key (cont.)

and they were tied together with ropes so that they wouldn't blow off the edge. If they had deserved the Medals, they would have gotten them.

Page 42

1. b   2. a   3. b
4. False. The world's tallest mountain lies on the continent of Asia. It is Mount Everest. OR False. The world's second tallest mountain lies on the continent of South America. It is Aconcagua.
5. Of the world's tallest mountains, the continent of Australia has the shortest one. It is Mount Kosciuszko, and it is 7,310 feet tall. Mount Cook is 12,315 feet high, so it is taller.
6. Yes, I would like to climb mountains because it sounds exciting/fun/interesting; I enjoy sports and hiking and I think it would be enjoyable; I like to challenge myself, etc. OR No, I would not like to climb mountains because it sounds difficult; it would take too much effort; climbing mountains is dangerous—look at what happened to Mark and Phil on Mount Cook, there are many ways to die while climbing such as falling, getting caught in a storm, freezing to death, etc.

Page 45

1. c   2. a   3. c
4. False. The monster wave occurred in the Southern Ocean. It surrounds the continent of Antarctica. OR False. The monster wave occurred in the Southern Ocean. The Pacific and Indian Oceans surround the continent of Australia.
5. There is a mesh filter inside the desalination pump. It traps the salt particles. Just the water comes out of the other side of the filter.
6. Yes, a desalination pump should be required on every ocean-going ship and boat. That way if something goes wrong and the people get stuck at sea, they won't run out of water to drink. OR No, a desalination pump should not be required on every ocean-going ship and boat. Large ships can carry all the fresh water they need. And if a boat sank, the person probably wouldn't have time to save the desalination pump anyway.

Page 48

1. b   2. c   3. c
4. True. While they were trying to drill a hole for the rescue cage, the drill bit broke. They had to start a new hole. It took many hours to fix this problem.
5. Three GPS satellite signals are needed to find a spot on Earth's surface. The place where they all intersect

is the location. The location is sent to a GPS receiver. When a person looks at the GPS receiver, he or she knows the location.
6. Yes, I would like to work in a coal mine. It sounds like an interesting job; my relative is a coal miner; it's one of the jobs available in our area; I wouldn't have to get a college degree to work there, etc. OR No, I would not like to work in a coal mine. It sounds scary and dangerous; the space in which the men had to work was small, and I don't like small spaces; I would hate being underground instead of out where I could see the sun and weather, etc.

Page 51

1. a   2. c   3. b
4. False. Even people thousands of miles away heard the eruptions. Those who died probably did not know that a tsunami was on its way toward them or didn't have anywhere to go to get away from the giant waves.
5. These are the names of villages completely destroyed by Krakatau. Anjer and Tjeringin were located on the island of Java, and Telok Betong was on Sumatra. The person sending the telegram from Batavia would be reporting about nearby places.
6. Yes, people should be allowed to live in areas with active volcanoes. After all, there are natural dangers in many settings. People are not told they can't live where there are numerous earthquakes, hurricanes, or tornadoes. Scientists now watch many volcanoes, and they may be able to give the people enough warning to escape. OR No, people should not be allowed to live in areas with active volcanoes. Nothing on Earth can stop a volcano from erupting, and when it does it will at the very least destroy people's property if not their lives. By living near active volcanoes, people know that they are putting themselves in danger. Then when the disaster comes, firefighters and rescue workers must risk their lives to save them!

Page 54

1. b   2. c   3. b
4. True. Two flags were posted to tell people of a coming hurricane and its direction. OR True. Two forecasters rode horses around the island telling the people to flee.
5. Debris/wreckage, 200 dead bodies/corpses, and a large steamship stranded on land could be seen from the train. (Any two)
6. Yes, it's wise for people to live in Galveston. It is a city, and many people make their homes there. Since

Answer Key (cont.)

they added the seawall, the island has never again been destroyed by a hurricane. OR No, it's not wise for people to live in Galveston. It is still just a sandbar and even though it has a good seawall, it can be broken by a bad enough storm. It's just a matter of time before another giant hurricane strikes and wrecks the island again. After all, New Orleans was protected by a seawall, and it was still destroyed by Hurricane Katrina.

Page 57

1. a   2. b   3. a

4. True. Trees provide a windbreak. They slow down the wind. Less wind means that less dirt gets caught up into the air. In fact, trees were so important that 18,500 miles of them were planted to restore the Dust Bowl.

5. The look on the farmer's face is one of discouragement, unhappiness, sadness, sorrow, despair, depression, hopelessness. He looks that way because he has lived in the Dust Bowl for years. His farm has been ruined. (Allow any of the adjectives given or their synonyms.)

6. Yes, the U.S. government acted quickly enough to help farmers in the Dust Bowl. The people in the government had no idea that the drought would be so bad or last so long (seven years). As soon as it became clear that the situation was an emergency, the Resettlement Administration was formed. OR No, the U.S. government did not act quickly enough to help farmers in the Dust Bowl. The drought started in 1931 and the Resettlement Administration began in 1935. Four years is too long for crops to fail! The government should have started helping out one year after the drought began. By then it should have been obvious that the situation was serious.

Page 60

1. c   2. c   3. a

4. True. Most people survived the earthquake. An avalanche triggered by an earthquake caused the terrible damage done to Yungay. OR False. In Yungay streets cracked and buildings fell down during the earthquake.

5. No. The advice given is for people on a mountain during a snow slide. The people of Yungay were not skiing or snowboarding and did not have rescue beacons. The avalanche in Peru was not a typical one. The people were in the valley and their slide contained boulders, water, mud, and trees as well as snow and ice.

6. Yes, I think it is fair because it's the resort's policy. It is clearly stated and was put in place to save lives. If the person doesn't want to wear the rescue beacon, then that person should go to another ski resort that doesn't require one. OR No, I do not think it is fair because the person has paid for the lift ticket. If people want to risk their lives by not wearing rescue beacons, then they should have that choice.

Page 63

1. b   2. a   3. c

4. True. The flood occurred on July 31, 1976, and the plaque states that it was dedicated on July 31, 1978. That's two years to the day.

5. The police officers were named W. Hugh Purdy and Michel O. Conley. Their names are shown on a plaque that honors them for trying to save others during the flash flood.

6. Yes, the officers that warned the people should have forced them to leave the gorge. By letting them stay, they created an emergency situation in which people and rescue workers died. I bet in the future when they suspect a flash flood is coming, they will force the people in the gorge to leave it. OR No, the officers who warned the people did the right thing by not forcing them to leave the gorge. The officers were not certain that a disaster was about to happen. And people in America have freedom of choice, even though that means that sometimes they make bad decisions.

Page 66

1. b   2. b   3. c

4. False. Scientists have several theories, but no one knows for sure. OR False. Scientists say that a landslide or a slight volcanic eruption may have caused it.

5. The names of the three lakes that have a carbon dioxide problem are Lake Nyos, Lake Monoun, and Lake Kivu. CO_2 stands for carbon dioxide.

6. Yes, the people living near Lake Nyos today are safe because now a fountain brings up a little carbon dioxide all the time so that a big bubble cannot form in the lake's depths. OR No, the people living near Lake Nyos today are not safe because no one knows what caused the first disaster. Perhaps the volcano under the lake will erupt. That could put them in danger. If there were another huge landslide, it could force the lake's water over its banks and flood the towns. The people are safer than before because of the fountain, but they are not completely safe.

Answer Key (cont.)

Page 69

1. a   2. b   3. c

4. False. I should not be using matches or fireworks if an adult is not present. Both flames and fireworks can be dangerous. Gunpowder can explode from a small spark. If it happened while I was close to it or holding it, I could be hurt.

5. Two uses for fireworks include celebrating, marking the scene of an accident, and notifying a train engineer that she or he must stop immediately. For celebrating, people set off fireworks as part of a festival because they are pretty. Flares are a type of red fireworks. They are set up to keep people from driving into a dangerous area. Railroad torpedoes are also fireworks. They blow up as a train runs over them to tell the engineer to stop the train. (Accept any two that include a description.)

6. Yes, people should be allowed to own guns because most people use guns responsibly. And if guns are outlawed, only the criminals will have them! Now if someone breaks into your home, he or she doesn't know if you have a gun or not. OR No, people should not be allowed to own guns because many people die in gun accidents and when someone loses his temper. If guns weren't readily available, there would be less crime. The police and the military need guns. The rest of the people do not.

Page 72

1. a   2. b   3. c

4. True. The article says that he borrowed money to make the press in 1448 and two years later printed his first book.

5. It took six steps to print something on the Gutenberg press. The third step was putting the galley tray into a metal frame called a type form.

6. Yes, the Worldwide Web will bring about the end of book publishing because it offers so much information for free. There are online dictionaries and encyclopedias, etc. Often the first place people turn to is the Web to find information on any subject. Information on the Web can be constantly updated, too. The information in books becomes dated. Eventually books will stop being made. OR No, the Worldwide Web will not bring about the end of book publishing because people like books they can hold in their hands. Many people don't like reading on a screen. Some people like to write in the margins or use highlighters on their books, too. Also, not every person has access to the Web. The Worldwide Web may reduce the number of books that are published, but it will not end the book publishing industry.

Page 75

1. c   2. c   3. a

4. False. In order to save his life, Galileo had to say that he had lied about the sun and planets in his book. If he had not said that he lied, he would have been put to death by the Church.

5. The planet closest to the sun is Mercury. The fourth planet from the sun is Mars.

6. Yes, Galileo should receive credit for inventing the telescope because he made the first useful one. It magnified things 32 times because he used curved lenses. The first telescope ever made was very crude and Galileo had to improve it in order to use it to study the sky. OR No, Galileo did not create the first telescope; a Dutch person invented it. Galileo made the first useful telescope with curved glass lenses, but he did not come up with the idea for the invention. He just figured out how to improve it.

Page 78

1. b   2. c   3. b

4. False. Mary Anning found skeletons of Ichthyosaurus, a Plesiosaurus, and a Pterosaur. OR False. Gideon Mantell (or his wife) found Iguanadon teeth and later bought its whole skeleton.

5. Gideon Mantell gets the credit because he wrote an article that told others about his discovery. Mary Anning was just a girl and did not write about her findings.

6. Accept reasonable responses, so long as the student offers a reason, such as this: I would like to see a stegosaurus because it would not eat me, and I think it looks neat with the rows of bony plates along its spine.

Page 81

1. b   2. a   3. a

4. True. First Lister started dressing wounds with carbolic acid. Then he cured sores and skin infections with it. Later he made a pump that sprayed carbolic acid to clean the air while an operation was going on.

5. The best thing I can do to keep from spreading germs is to wash my hands often. It is important for me to cover every sneeze and cough so that germs won't spread from me to another person through the air.

6. Yes, I will wash my hands more often. I never realized that washing my hands was the best way to keep from

Answer Key (cont.)

getting sick. I really hate being sick! And it's not hard to wash your hands; you just have to remember to do it. OR No, I won't wash my hands more often because I already wash my hands before eating and after sneezing. My mom/dad/teacher taught me to wash my hands often. Maybe since I keep my hands so clean, it's why I am hardly ever sick.

Page 84

1. a   2. a   3. c
4. True. Hoover states in its ad that it makes the largest-selling electric cleaner in the world. It also says that, "Only The Hoover does these things." Both of those statements make you realize that some other company must be making electric cleaners. (Accept either reason.)
5. In 1921, vacuum cleaners were called electric cleaners. Hoover called its electric cleaner The Hoover. (Accept either answer.) The ad says that vacuuming rugs will get buried dirt, lift crushed nap, and revive the color. It also states that using The Hoover will protect valuable rugs from avoidable wear. (Accept either answer.)
6. Yes, I like to use new gadgets because they make life easier; they are fun and interesting; I like to learn about/use new technology, etc. OR No, I don't like to use new gadgets because then I have to figure out how to use them; a lot of times it's easier to just do something yourself rather than figure out how to make the gadget do it; I don't like complicated things; etc.

Page 87

1. b   2. c   3. a
4. False. Plastics marked "1" can be used to make fabrics such as microfleece or fiber filling. OR False. Plastics marked "3" and "4" are mixed with plastics marked 5–7 and made into large plastic items such as pipes, lawn chairs, lumber, etc. (Allow any of the items from the last column of the chart for 3–7.)
5. Three kinds of plastic marked "6" are meat trays, egg cartons, cups, insulation, plastic forks, spoons, knives, and packing "peanuts." (Accept any three.)
6. I think that glass is the most important to recycle because it never rots. Once it's thrown in a landfill, it lasts forever and just takes up space. OR I think that metal is the most important to recycle because so many big things are made of it, like cars and appliances. OR I think that paper is the most important to recycle because it takes up more landfill space than anything else, and it would save the lives of trees. OR I think

that plastic is the most important to recycle because so many things are made of it, and plastic can so easily be melted down and made into new things.

Page 90

1. a   2. b   3. c
4. True. Most geysers are not predictable. That's what makes the Old Faithful geyser so interesting and famous—it erupts about every 77 minutes.
5. At the bottom, the melted rock heats the reservoir of water above it. This layer has a tube that connects to a reservoir of boiling water and steam just below Earth's crust. This top reservoir has a short tube. Steam and water shoot up through it when the geyser erupts.
6. I think geysers are the most interesting hot spots because they look beautiful when they erupt and as long as you don't get too close, they're not dangerous. OR I think volcanoes are the most interesting hot spots because when they erupt, they are dangerous and exciting. They spew lava, ash, and hot rocks and can form new islands. OR I think hot springs are the most interesting hot spots because even in the wintertime they let people soak in a "hot tub"; they are not dangerous. OR I think mud baths are the most interesting hot spots because I've never taken a bath in mud; people think that the mud baths can cure illnesses; they are not dangerous. (Allow reasonable responses.)

Page 93

1. b   2. c   3. a
4. False. Chuchan was "shoved into the fire" by the force of the blast. Chekaren was his brother and wouldn't push him into the fire. Chekaren was just as shocked and frightened as Chuchan by what was happening.
5. Chuchan says that he remembers hearing a total of five thunder strikes. They were caused by the explosion and not by a thunderstorm. He states that the sun was shining and there were no clouds in the sky.
6. I think that the eyewitness accounts are more important because they tell exactly what was seen and heard at the time the blast occurred. Their memories are like instruments that recorded the order in which things happened. OR I think that scientific observations are more important because there's no way that you can tell it was probably an asteroid by reading the eyewitness account. Knowing about the radiation and types of crystals lets scientists draw realistic conclusions. OR I think that eyewitness

Answer Key (cont.)

descriptions and scientific observations are equally important because what information one doesn't give the other might. There is no physical evidence left of the blinding light or the five thunder strikes that Chuchan mentions. But using his eyewitness account in combination with the scientific evidence (fallen trees around a central point, high radiation, crystals), scientists can drawn more definite conclusions.

Page 96
1. c   2. b   3. a

4. False. The river lay between the King and his adored Queen. People dashed between the two using boats. They could not use horses and carriages to cross the river until the bridge was built.

5. The Island Queen is the town of Brooklyn. The King of the Western Hemisphere is New York City. The silvery tie joining them is the Brooklyn Bridge.

6. Yes, bridge construction workers today would accept Emily Roebling as their leader. People are used to having women in leadership roles. And now there are women who work in construction, so the workers wouldn't find it odd if one was in charge of the project. OR No, bridge construction workers today wouldn't accept Emily Roebling as their leader. She was not trained or experienced in bridge construction. If the head of the project got sick, today's workers would expect a skilled replacement instead of the person's wife.

Page 99
1. c   2. a   3. c

4. True. Every new book that a library gets has its information put into the card catalog. When people search the card catalog, they find the title, author, publication date, and other information about the book. They will also discover where the book is shelved.

5. I would look under 598 to find books on different types of birds. I would look under 796.332 to find books about football. I would look under 912 to find an atlas.

6. I prefer reading fiction books because I like stories; I can picture myself living through the events in the book; I can visit other places and times; it helps me understand how others feel or how others deal with problems like mine, etc. OR I prefer reading nonfiction books because I like to learn about new things; I like to read about places, people, and events

that are real; it helps me to make good decisions—like when I wanted a pet, my parent made me read about how to take care of it so that I could be sure that I really wanted it.

Page 102
1. b   2. a   3. c

4. True. The lightships could not leave their posts no matter how bad the weather got. They had to stay in place to warn other ships of danger. As a result, storms sometimes damaged or sank lightships.

5. Just 10-11 minutes passed between the *Green Bay* striking the *Relief* and the lightship sinking. The *Relief's* crew fired flares, shouted, and tried to paddle toward the sounds made by the *Green Bay*.

6. Yes, the crew of the *Queen Elizabeth* saw the *Relief's* life raft. How could they have missed seeing 30 flares? The crew kept the big ship from hitting the raft. But it takes a long time to stop a big ship, and the captain probably felt that he would be unable to find the survivors in the dense fog. OR No, the crew of the *Queen Elizabeth* never saw the *Relief's* life raft in the thick fog. If they had seen it, the ship would have stopped to help. Ships do not just go past life rafts and do nothing. It was probably just luck that kept the ocean liner from hitting the life raft.

Page 105
1. c   2. b   3. a

4. False. Mount Rushmore is named after a New York City lawyer, Charles Rushmore. OR False. Mount Rushmore is not named after any president, but it has the heads of four famous U.S. presidents carved on it.

5. No, the faces will not wear away from weathering during my lifetime. The erosion rate is one inch every 10,000 years. Those faces will be there for a long, long time!

6. Yes, I would like to go see Mount Rushmore because I think it would be interesting to see the world's biggest sculpture; I like to travel and see new things; it would help me to imagine how the men made it, etc. OR No, I wouldn't like to go see Mount Rushmore because I don't like to travel; I am not interested in sculpture; I think seeing it on a computer screen or photograph is just as good as going there, etc.